The Courtiers
of
American Business

Also by W.T. Brahmstedt

Memo To: The Boss
From: Mack

THE COURTIERS
OF
AMERICAN BUSINESS

BY

(William T.)

W. T. BRAHMSTEDT

ETC Publications

C|P

Library of Congress Cataloging in Publication Data

Brahmstedt, W. T. (William T.), 1924 -
  The courtiers of American business.

  1. Success in business — United States.   2. Managing your boss.   3. Interpersonal relations.
  I. Title.

HF5386.B777   1987   650.1'3   86-29078

ISBN 0-88280-118-X

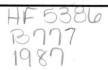

Copyright ©1987 by W. T. Brahmstedt

Published by ETC Publications
             Palm Springs
             California 92263-1608

CONTENTS

To the Seven
Out of Love — By Dominance

PREFACE

Two years have passed since I completed the writing of a contemporary rendering of *The Prince* by Niccolo Machiavelli. I titled the work, *Memo: To the Boss, From: Mack* (ETC Publications). Before the work was completed I realized that if the effort had value it was to be as a teaching tool for the uninitiated who enter the pursuit of life and must attain some degree of understanding of their enemies. The dedication of the work reflected that realization. The background for the writing was the corporate world, yet, the offering of Machiavelli, from whom the essence of the writing flowed, had major impact on many beyond his Princedom. My hope today is still, that *Memo: To the Boss, From: Mack* will have an offering beyond the corporate world to which it was directed.

The Courtiers, written by Baldassare Castiglione but fifteen years after *The Prince* was completed, has been throughout history a companion volume to Machiavelli's work. The impact of both writings have together influenced societies for almost four hundred years. Most commentaries on the two writings contrast their offering diametrically. Personally, I have always felt that they had much in common. The iron hand of Machiavelli and the gentility of Castiglione have one overriding similarity — reality.

In our American system of business today, the iron-handed method is frowned upon. Gentility has taken leave of our society to be replaced by ultimate individuality — where other's feelings are of little concern. On the surface the ironhanded approach is no longer used nor gentility practiced openly. Yet, in reality, the path to the top demands their inherent practice. Dream though we may as freedom-seeking Americans, the submission to will is still the only path to success. To conform, the method.

The system is the demanding force that belies any professed degree of individuality. To function within the system requires acceptance of that system's mode of operation. There is no way around it. At the top reside but few who control the destinies of those climbing the ladder through the system. Should any aspire to attain the top positions within the system, conformity is demanded. Proclamations of individuality followed by evident display of practice inhibit the path to fulfillment. Only those, who by strength of will and awareness of the demands of the system, will attain the levels within the system that offer the reward of the great American dream.

The products of our great American educational system are ill equipped as they depart the campus to cope with the reality that the system within the business community demands. The tools they acquire while in the halls of academia give little hope of success. The punishment they must undergo before realizing the true needs of the system retards, if not destroys, their incentive. Their mechanical expertise in any field is not sufficient to assure survival nor reach out to the rewards that the system offers. They are thrown into the system and left to their own devices. Many falter and fall by the wayside, who if given but a show of reality during their formative years could aspire and attain the highest levels of accomplishment that the system can draw forth from skilled participants. Such a waste!

The omission in the academic world lies in the forgetfulness that man needs more than mechanical skills to live among other men. He needs knowledge of men and what men expect of other men. He needs to be shown that there are rules to any game and the game of the system into which he is to enter are strict.

Castiglione was brilliantly aware of the need and set down for his generation a careful delineation of those rules. In that system in which he resided the arena was the court. To its attainment he schooled his Courtiers.

In our generation, and for those who wish to partake of its benefit within our system, we have replaced the court with the business community. To attain its upper levels, where the fruit of reward lies abundantly available, our aspiring participants must conform to the system's demand with the skills of a Courtier.

Castiglione's instructions are no less of value today than they were five hundred years ago. We only have to rephrase them into a language that is more comprehensible to our time. The writing that follows will hopefully attain that purpose.

Baldassare Castiglione, as painted by Raphael, dressed in the court style of the time.

INTRODUCTION

In the Board Rooms, Administrative Offices, Country Clubs, Racquet Clubs, Fancy Restaurants, Hunting Lodges, Yachts, and Brothels of American business, the would be Courtiers abound. They are as much a part of the scene as the Presidents, Owners, Stock Holders, and customers of any American business establishment. Their ranking in the pecking order of management starts at the supervisory level and travels through the entire management spectrum, reaching the pinnacle of attainment with Vice Presidential status. They are needed. They are wanted. They are used. They are vulnerable. How did they reach their present position? Who trained them? Who nurtured their growth? Who likes them? Who despises them? Who are they?

Until the Courtier attains the position of President or Owner, he may be called Flunky. The guy to be used. The one who is always about when needed. The one who does the right things at the right time to make President, Boss, or Owner, happy. The guy on the way up. The one who will do what is necessary to attain the end he feels is worthy of the doing. These definitions and many others, define him. Yet, he never knows, nor even considers that he bears the title. He considers all things as being necessary to do his job. If he is good at it — succeeds in attaining the end for which he aspires — he accepts the demeaning tasks as exemplary performance. The world in which he lives rewards only success. If attained, seldom is there question as to how. What was left along the way as residue is swept under the rug of forgetfulness and the pinnacle of accomplishment masks all previous effort. This is the system.

We do not normally think of this system as kindly, in any sense of the term. Yet, it is. The corporations that dominate our system are kingdoms, as surely as if established by royal blood. Each has its king and each has its retinue of Courtiers. These Courtiers are retained at the pleasure of the king and serve only when that pleasure is continually satisfied.

The President, Boss, or Owner of any corporation is kingly within his domain. The operation over which he rules, though not defined by territory, is no less worthy of the title kingdom than if it had borders of oceans or mountains, rivers, or deserts. His word within his domain is law. His wish, a command to the Courtiers on his payroll.

We may flinch at the term Courtier. Managerial staff members could no more consider themselves bearing this title than they could that of servant to a king, yet, their functionality in our system reflects clearly the reality of the title. Their own personal performance glaringly shows the similarity. There are differences, certainly, as there are differences between the kingdom of old and the corporation of today. The aura of kingdom is just as evident in the corporate arena today, as the pleasures of court life, with all its daily intrigue manipulating the course of history, was evident in the palaces of old. Each has its king. Blood or victory giving rule to one — ownership or votes giving life to the other. The similarities are easily related — the power factor most evident.

The Courtier, in the court of the king, was a servant. His power and position were attained not by his function in the hierarchy of the state but his ability to charm and gain favor. By so doing, he had influence — that immeasurable force that brought him into the inner circle of government and permitted his ideas to affect policy.

He was welcome at times of kingly discussion and when the need arose on the part of the king to explore avenues beyond his own initiative. He was a source. He was expected to entertain, in the sense of being adept at conversation and pleasantry. His pleasant-tongued attitude made his presence welcome at court and his demeanor added to the cultural heritage of the kingdom. He was a gentleman — comfortable under all circumstances — lending grace and ease to any gathering. He prided himself on his cultivated nonchalance, accepting challenge and burden with effortless ease. His rewards were grandiose.

In many cases, not of royal blood, his target could not be the top, but a position just beneath the king — with the power of the kingdom given for functionality — as reward. His word became that of the king and fear of his displeasure made him a ruler without the breeding of royalty. His tenure was determined by his ability to satisfy the king's need. His termination could be instant, given loss of favor by indiscretion.

The Courtier, on the staff of the President, Boss, or Owner, is a servant. His position was attained by pleasing the leader. His longevity is assured by continuance of that pleasure. Beyond the mechanical function under which he operates, he must assuredly guarantee satisfaction, gratification, and if need be, indulgence to the leader, if he is to survive. He must work diligently to gain favor, as did the Courtier of old, to assure his continuity and place him in position where his growth will flow from his ability to offer advice and assistance beyond the mechanical function for which he is paid.

Unlike the Courtier of old, today's Courtier has the potential for attaining the position under which he serves. He can be President, Boss, or Owner. Therefore, his challenge is greater and the potential reward more tempting.

Style is the unique quality of the Courtier and its diversity is unlimited in our contemporary business environment. Courtiers today are not trained, as were the Courtiers of old. They acquire their style from adapting. They see a niche in the corporate structure that appeals to their personality and they fill it. They are forever mobile. If successful in reaching positions of power and prestige, they adjust their demeanor and appearance to suit the capacity in which they have been placed. They are chameleons.

Unlike the Courtier of old, our Courtier has a much wider operational framework. Certainly, he is in evidence at the top or near it, but also, because of the complexity of our corporate system, we see him in operation at all subsidiary levels of management.

The absence of awareness of the title in those who practice the art of the Courtier is surprising. The performing of functions demanded, and not knowing that the effort is clearly designed within the system as a format to success, is most evident among our working force in the business community.

To identify them is first in importance-having them admit their position offers to them the opportunity of improving their proficiency. Many there are who will deny their efforts as being of the Courtier's doing. Such will be to their detriment.

Through the teaching of Professor Thomas Vernon, in the chapters that are to follow, his students will have the Courtier identified. They will realize that each of them has taken on the title and is performing the Courtier's function. Reluctantly, admission of reality will open their minds to improvement of their understanding and refinement of their method.

It is to the improvement of the quality of the Courtier and giving him the status he deserves, under the title he should bear with honor, that the effort of this work has been devoted.

WELCOME

Thomas Vernon walked into the classroom and sat down at his desk facing the students. There were six of them.

"Good afternoon. My name is Tom Vernon. First, let me thank you for coming to a class at three o'clock on Friday afternoon — not normally a fruitful request by any teacher. Having spent a week with difficult subject matter, a cool beer would be more welcome."

There were smiles from all and a comment or two of agreement.

"I will keep you here but a few minutes. Please bear with me."

Tom stood up and walked to the window that looked out onto the campus. A peaceful scene, now that summer session was in force. He could see only four students crossing the green, well-shaded lawn. The evident cool shade made the classroom they were in most unwelcome — almost depressing.

"If the weather is as favorable on Monday, as it is today, I think we should convene this class out under that big oak. Any objections?"

He turned to face the smiling faces. There were no objections and he had given a degree of relaxation to their evident feeling of uncertainty about himself and the course.

"Summer on the campus must be a time to enjoy the gift of nature, along with the burdens of academic offering. We will spend as much time outside as the weather will permit during the coming week. As you will see, our subject matter lends itself beautifully to such an environment. Our classes will not be confined by numbers on the clock. We are not here to give lectures or receive them. Our format is to be open. I mean that in the sense of full discussion by each of you throughout the five days we are together. As you know from your schedule, our classes will start at three o'clock, after your other commitments have been completed for the day. We have assigned a two hour time frame to the course but the nature of the discussions may extend that frame or diminish it, depending on the intensity you each acquire, as we pursue the subject. More on that phase of our course in due course.

"In a sense, you are fortunate to be the first group to be exposed to the course this summer. You are at the minute, free of any pre-judgment of its content. Your friends, who are scheduled to take the course throughout the summer, will not be so blessed.

"As you know, there are seventy-two of you here on campus for the twelve week program. Groups of six will give maximum opportunity for our needed open discussion. There are no charts, graphs, ledgers, or other writing material of any kind needed for the course. There are to be no lectures. I see no reason for you to take notes. My chore is to guide you in detailed discussion of the subject matter and nurture the understanding that will hopefully come to each of you within the five days that we will be together.

"You have attained some degree of proficiency at being Courtiers or your companies would not have chosen you for the program."

There was restless movement among the six. The word Courtier and the accusation that they were bearing the title did not set well.

"Obviously, you do not agree with that statement. The title 'Courtier' is not one that is used or even considered as being part of our current business community. We will change that impression within the next five days.

"This first class, from what has been given to me as information on your background, is composed of two Engineers, one Chemist, two Business Administration majors and one Journalist. A fine mix for our purpose. Your time of exposure in the business world is relatively short. The Chemist but a year and a half; one Business Administration major, three years; the others, somewhere in between. Each of you has seen the working of the business community and has attained some degree of Courtiership during that brief exposure.

"At this point, I feel certain you are not sure what the term Courtier means, as it applies to your efforts within your own company. Understandable. We will correct that uncertainty by giving you a reading assignment for the weekend — the primary purpose of this meeting today. The effort will take less than an hour, so that its reading should not interfere with your needed unwinding over the weekend — which I have no intention of disturbing.

"When you arrive at your first class on Monday afternoon — and we will initiate the class here in this room — you may be angry. You will feel that what I have given you to read is demeaning. But if you are honest with yourself and take objectively the examples given in the writing, I am certain you will see yourself and many others with whom you have had contact during the brief time you have been in the workplace.

"I must clarify one other point before you leave — my own position. As you have heard, I am not a full time member of the faculty here at the University, although I hold dear this campus and its facility, having obtained my own undergraduate degree here thirty seven years ago. I now have the luxury of being retired. I have taken on this assignment each summer for the past three years with the hope of offering to the graduate students, and to those like yourselves, who come in for advanced study, a clarification of the system under which you work.

"Suffice it to say, that I was a Courtier. What level of professionalism I attained will be yours to judge. I did manage to reach beyond the Courtier's realm and have the reward of carrying the President's responsibility at an international corporation for eight years, before stepping down at age sixty. My credentials will be yours to judge within the coming week of discussion.

"The study of the Courtier and his place in the system is not included in any standard curriculum. I feel, as do the Directors of the University, that it will be with time. Little is offered to students beyond their specialty during the four years of effort on the American campus. Having seen the workplace, as you have, the value of the present course will show its worth as we proceed through discussions. We are dealing here — in the fullest sense of the word — with reality, a subject that is not broached in the classroom, aside from its obvious nature in science. Its discussion with regard to people is not taught, and this omission we will attempt to correct. To work among people in the American marketplace requires a knowledge of functionality, just as certainly as do your efforts at your specialty. To this end we will direct our discussion.

"If there are no questions, this first class meeting is finished. We will meet for our first full session on Monday afternoon at three o'clock, here in this classroom."

Tom walked over to his desk and picked up a stack of blue folders.

"These are yours to keep. Please read the contents before we meet on Monday."

Each student thanked Tom as they took the folder. There was no offered commentary. They were uncertain. They left the room without further delay.

Tom smiled, as the last young man accepted his folder and walked out of the room. As he sat back down at the desk, he thought to himself, they will have questions on Monday — of that I am certain.

NOTE — Here, the reader should refer to the Appendix, Page 165, to read the contents of the Blue Folder given to the six students. Its subject matter will have a strong bearing on the questioning directed to Professor Vernon during the first day of class on Monday.

DAY ONE

THE IDEAL COURTIER

Tom Vernon left his office at one minute before three o'clock on Monday afternoon and started down the hall to the classroom. As he approached the entrance to the room, he could hear lively discussion from within. He hesitated briefly at the door and then stepped inside.

"Good afternoon, Gentlemen."

He heard two "Good afternoon" responses and then quiet, as he walked to his desk.

Glancing at the class and noting the number present, he sat down and set his copy of the Blue Folder in front of him.

"Would anyone care to volunteer the definition of a Courtier?"

All six of the students were looking at him but no sign of response appeared to be forthcoming.

"Possibly an unfair question at this point. Let it pass."

Tom stood up and walked to the window. It was raining and his thought of last Friday of convening the class outside came to mind.

"When we met briefly last Friday, I told you that this course was to be one of open discussion. I want that format to start now. I assume you have each read the Blue Folder I gave you and I am certain there are many questions arising from its content. Why don't you get them off your chest?"

"The characters described in this Blue Folder were either Flunkies or Ass Kissers."

The comment came from the student farthest back in the room. It was followed by others.

"You sure as hell can't respect them."

"Are we supposed to agree with them?"

"If that is the way to the top, I'm not sure I want any part of it."

"I'll buy that."

"That is one hell of a way to make a living."

Quiet. They had apparently run their course.

Tom walked back to his desk and sat down.

"Great," he said. "We now have your attention."

He leaned back in his chair and with an evident smile on his face repeated the words used by the first speaker with emphatic clarity, then added a few of his own.

"Flunky, Ass Kisser, Servants, Buddies, Tag-a-longs, Slaves, Climbers, Brown Nosers — let us remember those terms. We will be talking about them in depth over the next few days. But forget not, they are all to some degree would-be Courtiers.

"Before we go on, help me get squared away on your names and faces."

From the Blue Folder on his desk he extracted a sheet of paper.

"This thumbnail sketch they gave me on your background omits your job title. Would you please state it, as I call your name."

"Frank Johnson."

"Marketing Analyst."

"Everett Singleton."

"Process Engineer."

"Tim Powers."

"Product Design Engineer."

"Jack Hardy."

"Advertising Sales."

"Sam Cavanaugh."

"Analytical Chemist."

"Alec Martin."

"Associate Editor."

"Fine. Thank you." Tom said.

He made a last note on the sheet of paper and then looked up at the class.

"Everett Singleton — you have been in the workplace the longest. Do you deny seeing individuals in that workplace similar to those you read about in the folder?"

"Hell no. They are all over the place. There was nothing unique about the guys in the folder. The problem I have is that I don't see any reason to do what they do."

"You have a Boss," Tom said. "He may not be President but his position gives him power over your destiny. Have you not been nice to him over the last couple of years? Lighted his cigarette, opened a door for him, asked how his wife or kids were doing, given some indication that you were interested in him as a person?"

"Well certainly," Everett said, "but that doesn't put me in the class of being a Flunky. Those things are common courtesy."

"If he were an equal and you hated his guts, would you have done any different?"

"I don't think so," Everett answered with the first sign of uncertainty.

"To some degree, you wanted to have his friendship or at least his good will," Tom said. "Is that not true?"

"Yes, it's true but that doesn't make me an Ass Kisser does it?"

"Not the point," Tom said.

"What *is* the point, Professor?" The question came from Tim Powers.

"The point, Tim, is that we do these things without making distinctions in our mind as to why. They are natural responses in day-to-day contact with people. To those in authority, we condescend. Even in little things."

"You have us confused, with this term Courtier," Jack Handy said. "Really, Jack, it shouldn't be confusing. From what you read in the folder, you should have some idea of what we are about. Courtiers are not by definition Ass Kissers or any of the other names we have used for the position. They are members of a system. They take part in the system and perform functions that are necessary. You may question the term *necessary,* and be justified to a degree in many cases where an action is performed that does not seem to you to be worthy.

"Our first hurdle in this course is to get over the idea that the function of the Courtier is one of ass kissing or being some kind of Flunky. There are those in the system who deserve the title but they force themselves into the arena. They make everyone uncomfortable, especially the Boss or President . . . or any superior who has to deal with them. We will make clear distinctions about this breed as we go forward in our understanding. For now, try to consider in the term Courtier, those who are needed."

"Needed, or wanted by the Boss to be lackeys?" Sam Cavanaugh asked.

"Sam," Tom said, and then hesitated. "Have you been invited to lunch or golf as yet by any superior?"

"Yes, I play golf with the Sales Manager a couple of times a month."

"Are you in sales?" Tom asked.

"No, I am in the lab."

"Have you any interest in sales? Becoming a salesman?"

"I'd like it but haven't made an issue of it. Why?"

"Does the Sales Manager know of your disposition to sales?"

"I suspect he does. He hasn't brought up the subject."

"Why does he take you golfing?" Tom asked.

"He doesn't take me golfing. He heard I was good and invited me because he knew I enjoyed the game. He is damned good himself and we have some fine matches."

"Nothing else?" Tom asked.

"Like what?" Sam questioned.

"Chew on it." Tom said. "Alec Martin — how about you? Have you been to lunch, played golf, or done anything else in the extra-curricular area with a superior?"

Alec hesitated for a minute and then answered.

"I have been to lunch many times with my immediate boss and a couple of times with the Publisher."

"Were you needed at the lunches with the Publisher or were you along for good will?" Tom asked.

"What do you mean by needed?"

"Could whatever was accomplished at the lunch been accomplished if you had not been there?" Tom explained.

"I hadn't thought about it," Alec said.

"Jack Handy," Tom said with no further comment to Alec, "How about you?"

"I have been to the Boss' house for dinner."

"Did you take your wife?" Tom asked.

"Yes."

"Have you been back a second time?" Tom asked.

"Well, no. It was only about three weeks ago," Jack answered.

"Had you any contact with the Boss before the invitation?"

"I played tennis with him a few times at the club."

"Tim, how about you? Any contact with the Boss or President?"

"I know his daughter," Tim said sheepishly.

"Oh. How did you meet her?" Tom asked.

"You're getting kind of personal, aren't you?"

"Only enough to make a point," Tom said.

"I met her at the tennis club. She is a doll and I made it point to meet her."

"Any dates?"

"One."

"One more question, Tim, and I don't want you to answer it. Just think about it. Did you know she was the President's daughter before you approached her?"

Tim looked around at the other students but made no comment.

"How about you, Everett?" Tom asked.

"You have hooked just about everybody, haven't you?" Everett responded.

"Hooked is not the word, Everett. Admission is

30

the word. Are you ready?"

"Yeah. I have taken a number of trips with the Boss. I've carried his baggage. I've checked him in at the airport. I've parked the car while he went to make a phone call. What are you driving at, Professor?"

"Before we get into that, Everett, let's hear from Frank Johnson."

"I guess I'm suspect too," Frank said. "I live about two blocks from the President. I have had to pick him up mornings and take him home a couple of times after work. I have been asked to drop purchases and packages off at his house. Does that brand me a lackey?"

"In no way, Frank," Tom assured him.

"Now that we are all suspect," Everett said, "where do we go from here?"

"First and most important, you are not suspect," Tom said. "You are part of the system. It is the system that we are to explore. Your place in it will develop after we have attained an understanding of what the system is and how it operates."

"What about this Courtier bit?" Alec asked.

"That will follow," Tom said. "To some degree each of you is active in that system. Apparently, you have each performed with some degree of satisfaction or you would not have been chosen to partake of this summer program. The University does not put on this twelve-week program for free. It costs, and it costs big bucks. Your companies have agreed to spend those bucks as an investment in their future. Your future is also under development. You must ask yourself if you were chosen solely for the mechanical job you have done over the past one, two, or three years, or was your personality and adaptability to the system taken into account. I am certain that each of you has offered more to his company than just a great mechanical aptitude in whatever field you pursue. This is distinctly to your advantage and you should be pleased with your choice and grateful for the opportunity, knowing that when you return to the scene you will be better equipped to move with that lovely feeling of upward mobility that we hear so much about."

"Are you planning to make Courtiers out of us in five days?" Everett asked.

"I don't have to. You already are Courtiers," Tom answered. "I'm not sure I'll buy that name," Tim said. "It has the sound of something devious."

"Tim," Tom said, "that is just why this course was initiated. The activities we have spoken of here and what you read over the weekend in the Blue Folder, as well as many other examples we will discuss before we part, have been going on for years. They will continue to be practiced. They are part and parcel of American business. What we hope to do by discussing them in open format is to elevate their level of awareness and give to them the justification they deserve. To have shame attached to the doing is wrong. Granted, there are shameful practices going on in business and we will look at them later, as I mentioned to Jack, but they should in no way inhibit the progress of the legitimate Courtier. He performs a service that is as much needed in business as any expertise he may have in the field for which he has dedicated his life's effort. His expertise in that field will only assure him of his income for the day he does the work. If he does not join the system, and joining here means the sharpening of the Courtier's edge, he will have no assurance of his future growth.

No one has ever climbed the ladder in business by hiding in a cubbyhole.

"Let us try and justify what I have said. The Blue Folder contained a number of examples. Pick one or more that were most difficult to buy and we will discuss them. Everett, which one turned you off?"

"There wasn't any single example that bothered me. It was the idea of people being used. Take the example of the guy talking to his wife about who was going on the boat with him . . . he was more concerned about having a good crew than he was about giving pleasure to anyone by asking them to join him for a day on the water. He also was cocksure that anyone he asked would accept without question, and jump, even if it meant changing plans of their own. That is sick."

"Do all of you feel the same about this particular case?" Tom asked.

Only Frank did not agree. He made no comment at all.

"Frank, you seem to have some doubt," Tom said.

"I can see the reason for needing a good crew. My dad had a boat and he wouldn't take anyone out that could not be of some help. I don't like the idea of the assurance of every employee jumping at the Boss' offer. I think Everett is right on that score."

"Let us pursue the crew needs first," Tom said. "A man has a boat that he prizes highly. He has worked most of his life to obtain the means whereby he can pursue an activity that he enjoys. The boat has become a member of his family. His wife enjoys it. His children, when they are permitted to go on board, enjoy it. The man has great pride in the boat.

"The boat is of a size that requires more than one pair of hands to sail. Whenever he takes the boat out he must have someone, or depending on its size, a number of hands available to be assured of its safe handling. He plans a weekend trip with one or more nights on board. He and his wife agree that the trip should be with adults, so they decide to invite two or more couples to join them. The owner of the boat knows he cannot rely on women or at least he assumes that he cannot, so he must rely on the men he invites to give him a hand on board. Is it not logical to select from among his friends, couples that can be of assistance?

"Like most of us, he may not have a wide enough acquaintanceship or knowledge of assured or skilled hands to make a comfortable selection of guests. He works in a business that has a large number of employees. Many on his staff are qualified to be hands on board the boat. Is it not logical to fill up his crew with some of his employees? Certainly he is aware that most of the employees he would consider do not have a boat of the size of his, even if they might have a boat of their own. Any boat owner or lover of the water and sailing would certainly welcome the opportunity to spend a day or two on a comfortable vessel."

"Up to this point, Professor," Jack said, "you make sense. Enjoying a day on the water on a good boat is fine. Helping with the running of the boat is fine. That doesn't handle the idea of all the employees jumping when the Boss makes a request for crew members."

"All of the employees are not to be considered, Jack," Tom responded. "Only those who the Boss knows as Courtiers."

"What do Courtiers have to do with being potential members of the crew of the Boss' boat?" Sam asked.

"Go back in your mind to your own company," Tom said. "Think of each of the members of your staff — those with whom the President of the company has contact. Can you think of at least one that you would not want to be a companion on a weekend boating trip that you were to be part of?"

"Well certainly," Jack said, "I can think of a couple of guys I wouldn't want along."

"How about you, Frank?"

"Yes, I know of one guy I wouldn't want on a boat trip of any kind."

"Don't you think the Boss has the same feeling?" Tom asked. "He looks over his staff for potential guests, and certainly he has many whom he cannot consider. He does have a few that are of a nature to be worthy of invitation. His awareness of their value has come from contact and other personal relationships developed over some period of time. It is from among these that he must select or choose the right combination of companionship and ability to aid in the handling of his boat."

"Okay," Sam said, "but how do you justify his statement that they will all jump at his request?"

"As I said, he knows his Courtiers. They are men who know the system and make themselves available. They like boating, or at least he knows which of them do, and they are ever anxious to accompany the Boss on any pretext. They want and need his friendship. Is there a better way to get it than spending two or three days on his boat?"

"We need more discussion about this 'want and need' of the Boss' friendship bit," Alec said.

"We intend to have a great deal of discussion about it, Alec. It is the essence of the Courtier. Can you at least, at this point in our consideration of the crew choice, see the logic of the selection process?"

"If we assume those being considered Courtiers, as you put it," Tim answered, "those guys are after something. I am not sure I fully understand what."

"They are after the same thing you are," Tom responded. "They want upward mobility. They want a bigger piece of the pie. They want success."

"You're telling us, that if we want to move up in the company, we have to know how to be a crewman on somebody else's boat?" Frank commented.

"Only one example, Frank. There are many others. Can we hold further discussion of the crew choice for a minute?"

"Yeah. Let's get back to this 'want and need' of the Boss' friendship idea," Everett said.

"The way to approach that concept, Everett, is to first ask the question, 'Who is the Boss?' Follow this by another question, 'What is a Boss?' From answers to these questions we will find the answer to the need and function of the Courtier."

"Aren't these questions rather self-evident in any company?" Alec asked.

"Not really," Tom responded. "You can certainly identify the man with the title. Does the title tell you anything about the man himself? Obviously, not. If you wish to understand the method practiced by a Boss, it becomes imperative that you attain some degree of knowledge of his personality. This knowledge cannot be obtained at arms length. Contact is necessary. Such contact comes from personal relationships. From the most insignificant meeting in the hall to pass the time of day, to a weekend on his boat to enter into his private life. Full understanding comes from knowledge of his dreams and objectives."

"Why in the hell do we need to know his dreams

and objectives?" Jack asked. "We have our own."

"That question, Jack, leads to the answer to the question, 'What is a Boss?'" Tom responded. "Is he not the instrument by which your own dreams can be turned into reality? Does he not have the power to place you in position to rise to those dreams?"

"He is not God," Tim commented.

"No, he is not," Tom answered, "but he does have, within the workplace of your effort, power over the life or death of those dreams. He can fire you or he can move you upward through the organization to the position where those dreams become reality."

"That is pretty cold analysis," Everett said. "What about our ability? Is it of no value?"

"Your ability to perform the function for which you were hired is an expected commodity," Tom answered. "Your degree or training before the fact of joining the company has established your credentials. Our efforts here have no bearing on those credentials. It is assumed that they have been firmly established and that in your everyday effort on the job they will shine forth with the value they have been given by placing your name on the payroll."

"You are telling us," Everett said, "that our training is not enough. We have to acquire something beyond what the training gave us. With training alone, we will not succeed?"

"You must ask another question, Everett, and a question that will hopefully lead to the understanding of the Courtier. What is success?"

There was no immediate response to the question. Tom could visualize the range of responses being put together by each of the students. Their range of consideration was certainly subject matter for lengthy discussion. He did not wish to get into the consideration of dreams, so he took up the answer himself.

"Take the training of a Stationary Engineer. He is the man who sits for eight hours a day monitoring the dials and gauges on a boiler in a boiler room. He adjusts the flow of water and oil to the boiler by those dials and gauges. He maintains the pressure in the boiler to assure its maximum performance. He also maintains the cleanliness of the boiler room and prepares his charge for periodic inspection. His position is critical to the function of the operation that the boiler serves. He is a necessary part of the company, yet in the course of a year he may see the Boss or President only on a rare occasion. He reports to some person at an intermediate level who possibly knows nothing about his job or its demands. As long as the boiler functions to expected norms, his work is seldom recognized. He comes up for adjustment in salary at designated times and receives them, if his performance has been satisfactory. He is isolated from the other members of the operation solely by his location in an isolated area of the facility. How does he measure success?"

"By not blowing up the plant, I would suspect," Jack answered.

"A guy in that kind of a job has no ambition," Frank said.

"I had an uncle who was a boilerman," Everett said. "He raised a couple of kids and put them through college. I see nothing wrong with that job. It gave him a good income and he seemed real contented. I must admit that I don't think I could do it. Too boring."

"Was he successful?" Tom asked.

"By his definition," Tim responded, "I suppose he was."

"Aside from his contact with the person who hired

him," Tom said, "his training was sufficient to perform the job adequately. His agreement with the isolation of the job and his perseverance in doing it were all that was required to fulfill the responsibility. He was content in retaining the position and building a life from its return. He had neither desire for upward mobility or none was available. In any case, he served the company well and in so doing secured his position. His training was totally sufficient to fulfill the need required."

"If the President of his company had a yacht big enough to be driven by a steam engine," Frank said, "he might have been asked to go along as part of the crew."

"An unlikely possibility," Tom said, "but yes, within the context of a needed Courtier."

"His personality would have no bearing on his selection, either," Frank commented. He would certainly not have time to socialize with any of the other guests. He would be stuck in the boiler room. Not a pleasant outing."

"But he would be needed," Tom reminded them. "And as such, would add to the security of his position."

"This is getting kind of wild," Everett said. "Calling a boilerman who spends eight hours a day stuck in some hole in the cellar of a factory, a Courtier, because he is called upon on occasion to accompany his Boss to watch the boiler on his boat."

"The example is both unique and fruitful, Everett, as it has made a point and given you the need to use the word Courtier. Obviously, it is unlikely that a boilerman would ever encounter such a set of circumstances. The absense of the function of the Courtier in the position of boilerman requires some awareness of what the Courtier is. We are making progress. Let us go to another example of the non-Courtier and utilize a much more demanding level of training.

"The recipient of a doctorate in botany is enthralled with the development of a certain specie of plant. It has a potential for offering to the medical profession an extract that could be of substantial value. Both industry and the government realize the potential and our newly doctored scientist is given the means to fulfill his dream of further study by granted finances that permit him to travel to the jungles of the upper Amazon and set up a facility to pursue his objective. He hires natives to clear land and build the necessary structures to house a laboratory and other facilities. Equipment is sent in and he initiates the research project. His dedication is complete. His reports are mailed out with the necessary samples for further work on the project here in the States, at both the supporting government and industrial facilities. He has no contact with any of his superiors other than by mail. His project lasts for years. His reward is purely scientific advancement in an area to which he is dedicated.

"Like our boilerman, he spends his life in isolation. Upward mobility offers no incentive. He is content to pursue his studies and reap the reward of gained knowledge."

"He doesn't have to be nice to anyone," Tim said. "He can do as he damned well pleases, living in the jungle. Sure as hell, he is not going to be invited to go along for a boat ride with his Boss."

"He could sure be entertaining, if he did go along. I'll bet he could tell some great stories," Frank commented.

"Not the point, Frank," Tom said. "The point is that he has not the need of association with his Boss. Therefore, he need not develop the attributes of the Courtier."

"This Courtier we are searching for," Jack said, "seems to exist only where there are lots of people to compete with. He is not found in a boiler room nor in the jungle."

"He is not found where there is lack of potential for competition." Tom said. "This is the point of the examples of the boilerman and the jungle scientist."

"This word competition you just used," Everett said, "brings in a new idea. We have been talking about training, need for acceptance, friendliness with the Boss. Is competition the key?"

"In a sense, it is," Tom answered. "To be in the workplace and seek advancement is a game. Some are good at the game. You have heard the term gamesmanship. It is played by all who work and seek advancement. To play the game requires being among people. The isolated boilerman and the jungle scientist are not among people, therefore they do not need nor desire to take part in a game. To most, the game demands getting along with your fellow employees. To the one seeking upward mobility, getting along is only a small part of the plan for success. There is more — much more — to climbing the rungs on the ladder that lead to the top. The skills demanded are those of the Courtier. Skills that have no bearing on the mechanical training that placed the player in the game."

"In other words," Sam said, "anyone who is ambitious is a Courtier?"

"Not really, Sam," Tom responded. "Ambition alone is not sufficient. Certainly, it is a driving force. There are many who are ambitious that have little success, due mostly to their method or approach to the system. They aggravate rather than lend comfort to any situation. This type seldom attain any status, nor move up through an organization. Usually, they try too hard and foul up their own efforts by irritation."

"I know a few of those," Alec said. "Always in the middle of any conversation, with absolute knowledge of every damned thing being discussed. The maddening thing is that you can't get rid of them."

"If you feel that way about them, Alec, how do you think,they set with the Boss?"

"I doubt if he would invite them for a boat ride," Alec laughed.

"You're narrowing down this Courtier bit, aren't you," Everett said.

"By exclusion," Tom said. "But think — you are each still in the running — are you not?"

"Are we supposed to put signs on our desks that identify us?" Tim asked.

"How about name tags?" Jack questioned. "Cute. 'I'm a Courtier.' Maybe we should buy ties and have them monogrammed."

"Do I see signs of admission?" Tom asked. "Or, are we still at the stage of hesitancy?"

"Well, I didn't find anything in that Blue Folder you gave us that would make me very proud of being a Courtier," Alec commented.

"But you did admit to an action that falls well within the function of a Courtier," Tom said. "Weren't those lunches you attended designed to be of pleasure to the President?"

"I didn't know why I was invited," Alec said.

"I'll lay you good odds that you have done a lot of speculating as to why," Tom said. "I'll also do the same with regard to your desire for continuance of the practice."

"I like the recognition," Alec responded. "And besides, the Boss is fun to be with."

"You sound like you would like to invite him to lunch," Tom needled.

"I'm not that close to him. He is still the Boss."

"But you're working on it," Tom said.

"Does that mean that I'm a Courtier?"

"Yes, and apparently one who has acquired a measure of expertise," Tom answered.

"But damnit, Professor," Jack said, "the things you are holding up to us as functions of a Courtier are just the normal activities of people in business."

"Most of the things you are using as examples are not planned," Tim said.

"Guys like Alec don't plan to have lunch with the Boss," Frank said. "Things like that just happen. I don't plan the picking up of packages at the Boss' house. Tim didn't go looking for the Boss' daughter. The whole thing seems like a fabrication of what is no more than normal happenings. You appear to be putting design on every activity that takes place in the business community."

"In a sense, I am," Tom responded. "There are, however, selected limits. Much of the day-to-day activity you speak of is outside of the Courtier concept. What we are seeking by example and awareness are the causes that have design, designs that stem from the needs of the Boss or President . . . design by an employee who is aware of the potential for improvement in position, by being equipped and available in time of those needs. This is the concept we are exploring. This is the strength of the Courtier. This is what separates the true Courtier from the average employee. The average employee goes through business life with no awareness of how he may, with minimum effort, improve his position and potential by adjustments in his personality offering or his demeanor, when in a position to function as Courtier. It is this distinctive awareness that is paramount to reluctant success.

"Alec didn't design a plan for lunch with the Boss but when it happened he made his presence an asset and conducted himself in such a manner that he was welcome and assured the possibility of future invitations. Frank didn't ask to pick up a package at the Boss' house but something in his personality drew the attention of the Boss to have him make the choice of Frank over someone else. Tim did not meet the Boss' daughter because the Boss brought her to the plant for his pleasure. He was at the club where she happened on the scene — as he did — but by so doing the result was fruitful.

"Three words come to the fore from what we have been discussing — need, ambition, and competition. Need has been ascribed to the Boss but it resides as well with the courtier. Ambition is part and parcel of any consideration of a Courtier. Competition is what makes him tick. They all reside within the activity of the opportunist. The Courtier is without question, the supreme opportunist. The distinction we will make in our analysis of him and his function will remove from that word the connotation of repugnance and replace it with one of esteem.

"By your very presence here in this classroom, as part of a selected group of employees chosen to further their value to the company — who incidentally is picking up the tab for the course — you each clearly have captured the attention of your Boss, whoever he may be or whatever title he carries. His need for you is evident. Your need for his grace is clear. Your ambition has made your selection possible. Your ambition will make you more valuable employees. Your selection resulted because you attained a higher grade than others in your company in the way you presented your assets. You competed and won. Could you have attained the result without grasping the opportunity? No. You are, by admission, opportunists."

There was no response. Tom noted that Tim was making notes for the first time.

"Tim, you seem to be troubled. A problem?"

"Not really. I just wrote down a few of the words you have been using. Need, ambition, friendliness, competition, opportunity, and I was just about to write Ass Kisser."

"Flunky would be a better choice," Everett commented.

"You seem to be trying to make us feel like jackasses," Tim said. "If what you say is true, Professor," Alec said, "what must the employees back in the office think of us?"

"Let me quote," Tom said. '. . .a feeling of discontent and ill-will because of another's advantages, possessions, etc. . . . .' That is the dictionary definition of the word 'envy.' "

"You don't feel that Ass Kisser or Flunky have any part in this concept of Courtier?" Sam asked.

"None whatsoever," Tom answered. "I mentioned earlier that there were many in any organization who tried to feather their nest by inappropriate means that grated upon the Boss and others in the organization. I said then that we would talk about them later. Let's do so now and clean up that note you are writing,

Tim."

"Fine. At this point I need to get rid of this feeling of being guilty," Tim responded.

, "There is no need for guilt, Tim. Performance of honest effort need have no guilt. The guilty, and they do not have the feeling, are the Ass Kissers and Flunkies you just mentioned. Identifying them is not difficult. They do not act out of need or even request. They volunteer or force themselves into the doing of all manner of chores for their superior. Seldom are they asked to do anything. They stand around, or more realistically snoop around, looking to serve. To volunteer is their greatest challenge. They have no class. In many ways their presence is obnoxious. They can tell the foulest stories and get embarassed laughs. They force themselves into all kinds of meetings and social gatherings and in so doing make for discomfort. Many are hard to dispose of. If they survive in an organization, it is because their mechanical expertise is useful. Seldom, however, do they move up the ladder to positions of substance. I am certain that each of you can identify many within your own company."

"I know a few." Sam said, "but what bothers me now, is why does the Boss suffer their actions?"

"He is human," Tom said. "He likes to be served. He likes to have servants. There are many jobs that he would ask no one to do but if he regularly gets volunteers to perform them, why should he object?"

"You don't think these volunteers, as you call them, do themselves any good?" Jack asked.

"Not in the sense of advancing their position within the company, in terms of what is good for the company," Tom answered. "Oh, they will get improvements in income as needed. They will have a strong presence on a day-to-day basis but they will not be thought of in terms of grooming for upward mobility. They have a niche to fill and it is one that satisfies the personal needs of a Boss. Always, they are kept a safe distance from the significant. The fringes are their domain. You have each given them names — Ass Kisser, Flunky, Brown Noser — and there are many others. Over years of watching and seeing many come and go, I have given them a more definitive handle — condoned."

"Thinking back to the Blue Folder you gave us, Professor," Everett said, "do you admit that some of the actions of the characters used were appropriate?"

"Each has to be determined on its own merit, Everett," Tom answered. "There is a fine line of judgment in each of the cases presented. I would ask you to read them again tonight and attempt to make that judgment based on our discussion today. You must keep in mind the ever present humanness of a Boss, whether he be President or have any other position of authority. Ask yourself, is this character being developed for more useful purposes or is he being condoned. The Courtier, as we will more clearly define him over the next few days, does not fall into this category. He resides among the condoned but is not *of* the condoned. He assures his position and his future by being able to make the subtle distinction of what is right and what is demeaning. Never will he behave in a way that detracts from his growing stature as a proud member of the company from which he seeks the success that all desire. Our efforts here in the next few days will assist in giving you the tools that will make these judgments possible and fruitful."

"It would seem that there is a pretty damned fine

line between Ass Kisser and what you are calling Courtier," Frank commented.

"It is far less fine than you would suspect," Tom answered. "The task ahead of you is to be able to find that line and know on which side you wish to reside. The Courtier is an asset. He is needed and necessary for any company to grow, as he becomes part of the foundation upon which that growth develops. Placing yourself among the group that is to be a part of the growth of the company is necessary. To advance the company's objectives, demands knowledge of what is required of the Courtier and development within your own personality of the skills that will make a Courtier's performance outstanding. The ease of the identification of the condoned will improve as we proceed to hone the skills of the true Courtier. His faults will stand out like the thorns in the proverbial ass of progress, making your identification of him quite simple and by the doing, show the true value of the approach of the Courtier."

"Based on numbers, Professor," Alec said, "it would seem that what you call the condoned, far outnumber the Courtiers."

"No question about it, Alec. The key to the number situation is most evident when you look at the top staff in any company. The numbers are very small in relation to the total number of employees. The top positions in any organization are few in number. The line to those slots is also small, made up of a relatively few selected individuals who are chosen long before they reach a level of significance, as regard decision-making capability. These are the Courtiers. They have a quality, admittedly difficult to define, that places them among the chosen. The quality is not attained during their educational experience in formative years.

It is developed by careful choice, as they are exposed to the system. They are aware. This asset, *awareness,* is without doubt their most revered commodity. Their expertise in their mechanical training certainly has to be exemplary to justify their being kept on the payroll. With it, they can survive. With it alone, they remain cogs in a state of suspended animation, if you will, as they do not attain the upward mobility that you all so frequently refer to in your consideration of the system."

"Professor, I'll admit, I suspect the others will do likewise, that what you have explained in the last hour or so makes sense and I feel we have a handle on the Courtier concept," Everett said. "What now comes to mind are the exceptions. Guys that make it to the top and are true Assholes. I'm sure we all know a few."

Everett's statement caused a complete change in attitude in the room. Relaxation seemed to take over. Each made a comment and changed position. Sam got up out of his chair and walked to the window. Tom was pleased. He had them finally in the frame of mind necessary to proceed with the substance of the course.

Sam turned from the window and with a broad grin looked at Tom.

"You know, Professor, I'm certain my own Boss is an Asshole. Sure as hell he was never a Courtier. The guy is a jerk."

"Is he President?" Tom asked.

"No, just V.P. of Marketing."

"How did he get the job?" Frank asked.

"I sure as hell don't know," Sam said.

"Is he married to the President's daughter?" Alec asked.

"No, and I have no idea how he got up the ladder. Neither does anyone else."

"It is possible he holds some indiscretion over the President's head," Tom suggested. "A most useful tool in the course of progress."

"You mean that somewhere along the line he acquired a weapon?" Sam asked.

"That is one way of phrasing it," Tom said. "But remember one thing. Guys that attain positions using that approach do not really have security. Their Boss, whoever he may be, is somehow planning a way to dispose of him. He walks on tenuous ground. He is not an asset to the company in the long term, and any honest leader will at some point have to eliminate him. From where you observe a situation of that nature, it appears that the guy is golden. If the company is to grow with a long term future, assured by solid internal structure, a person of that nature is a detriment. He cannot be trusted nor given significant decision-making authority. He will, in time, be disposed of."

"That is small consolation, Professor," Tim said, "if the guy happens to be your Boss or is between you and the target job you are after."

"True, and keep in mind that the road ahead of you will be strewn with such roadblocks," Tom responded. "But keep in mind, also, that this country of ours offers ample opportunity for the true Courtier. Why do you think there is such active movement of personnel among companies? The movement is not solely by those who have been dismissed or released because their need has been canceled. Good men are always in demand. A roadblock of the type you mentioned, Tim, is very common and demands the search for other paths to the top. If you will look about your own particular business arena, you will note that there are very few top slots filled with men who have come to that level within that particular company. Upward mobility has the unique demand of well diversified experience. To attain the top of the ladder by having spent time at more than one company is quite acceptable. What is not acceptable is to have a string of moves on your resume. Too many changes generate questions of your own ability to become part of a team. To a manager searching for new blood, such a condition will become a roadblock of your own making."

"In the Blue Folder there are many examples, Professor," Alec said, "You asked us to read it again tonight and make an attempt to separate the Courtiers from the non-Courtiers. As I remember from my reading of the folder, the distinction is not going to be a simple one. We have talked about a Courtier's functions, his needs, his desires, his efforts, yet I don't recall you giving a definition of a Courtier."

"To be honest with you, Alec," Tom said, "I'm not sure I can. Certainly, not in a few words of concise meaning. The word Courtier has specific meaning, as I'm sure you can find in any dictionary. The word is one of ancient usage. The Courtier resided in the courts of Princes and Kings. He served at the pleasure of the Prince or King. His need was based upon his own abundant qualifications — at the time — clearly defined. He was well educated. He was proficient in arms and the manly arts. He was a wonderful conversationalist. He was welcome at any gathering for his ability to enlighten, entertain, or, as he grew in stature and grace, to advise. For his prowess and effort, he was generously rewarded by the Prince or King. His effort brought not only monetary reward but prestige, and ultimately power.

"Our use of the term is obviously different — yet, not in so great a degree that we lose the basic idea of the man and his objective. Our selection of the term Courtier more nearly fits the method of approach to attainment of an objective than it does the objective itself. By definition we have no Courtiers in our system, as did the Princes and Kings of old. We do have in our system the need for the Courtier's ability. At the end of the Blue Folder, if you recall, there was a parallel given. It was an attempt to compare the Courtier with a Salesman. Within this idea lies the definition you seek. A Courtier has vision. He has ambition and a clear awareness, and willingness to attain the equipment demanded to pursue that vision. You might define him as a realist within the system."

"You persist in omitting any discussion of what you have so frequently referred to, as mechanical training," Sam commented. "Has it no bearing on the definition of the Courtier?"

"Not really, Sam. Courtiers reside in all fields of endeavor. Certainly, we can find a Courtier in a woodworking shop, a pipefitting establishment, any manufacturing facility, a newspaper office, a government department, or a nuclear energy plant. I'm even sure we might look about us here in the world of academia and find a few."

"What about his upbringing?" Jack asked. "Does that have a bearing on whether a person can be a Courtier?"

"It has a great deal to do with it," Tom answered, "as does his personality. If, in his early training, awareness and reality have been instilled into the growth of personality, the path to Courtiership is more easily attained."

"Where does the knowledge of what a Courtier must acquire come from?" Everett asked.

"Unfortunately, Everett, there is no defined source. It is this omission that has led to the formation of this course. The knowledge required to function as Courtier is attained in our system solely by osmosis. More to our detriment as a business community, it is not even discussed. As you have seen in just the last couple of hours, the subject raises all manner of sarcasm and finger pointing to those whom we have so aptly named Ass Kissers, Flunkies, or Brown Nosers. To make the necessary distinction between these and the true Courtier demands honest discussion, such as we have had here. Once the concept of the Courtier is in place and the full benefit seen, we can proceed to offer instruction on the skills demanded and the honing of those skills to benefit self and the organization."

"Is this where we are headed in the next few days, Professor," Jack asked.

"Exactly," Tom answered.

"Do you plan to let us in on all your secrets?" Jack asked, with a broad grin.

"I'll try, but I must forewarn you; you are not going to like some of the offerings," Tom responded.

"It should be interesting," Everett said.

"Let's call it a day," Tom said. "Give those Blue Folders another read before tomorrow."

"How about class outside tomorrow?" Sam asked.

"If the weather is good, fine. I'd enjoy it and our discussion is as appropriate there as here. That big oak in the square can get mighty attractive on a warm day. We'll meet there if it shines."

The six got up and left the room — each offering

a friendly farewell to Tom. Their attitude had changed to one of resolve. He was pleased.

DAY TWO

THE IDEAL COURTIER

Tom was seated at his desk in the large third floor office assigned to him for the summer. The desk had been cleaned out but there were many articles still in the room that belonged to the permanent occupant. Pictures on the wall — a flight of ducks, a wilderness scene, hunters standing with guns and geese in hand — gave evidence to the occupant's hobbies. He knew that the man was a professor of biology and that he had taken the summer to study wildlife along the Gulf of Mexico, especially the species that did not migrate north. Glass cases lined the walls of the high ceilinged room and their contents ran from seashells to preserved ducks and other waterfowl. An interesting room. It would be great to meet the man who occupied it during the regular school year.

He picked up the Blue Folder from the desk. He gave it one more brief review, then set it down. He did hope that each of the students had gone over its contents again last night. He rose from the desk and noted from the large clock over the door facing him that it was quarter to three. At the window that looked out over the square of the campus, his eyes went to the large oak alongside of the opposite end of the building, just beneath the window of their assigned classroom. He was surprised to see the six students already lounging on the grass.

They are early, he thought to himself. I hope it is because they are interested. No sense in keeping them waiting.

He went to the clothes rack in the corner of the room and took down his jacket. He paused in the process of putting it on and returned it to the rack.

I don't need the formality of a jacket out on the grass, he thought to himself. No classroom today. And besides, it is hot.

He approached the desk to pick up the Blue Folder, but again changed his mind. He left the room empty-handed, loosening his tie as he proceeded down the hall.

As he stepped out of the building, the students seemed to come to attention — not rising, but each sitting up to watch his approach.

Walking toward them, he noted that the Square was essentially unoccupied — only three other students in view. The late afternoon timing of his course was a distinct asset. They would have no attention loss due to passing bodies.

The Square was not extensive. Two hundred feet on each side and a building abutting the four quadrants. The buildings were almost identical and at the corners arches directed paths to and from the tree covered lawn. A full enclosure. Lovely in the summer and a most protective environment from bitter winds in winter.

Sam, who had been leaning against the tree, stood up as he approached and was the first to greet him.

"Here, Professor, take the seat of honor. At least you will have a backrest."

"How is everybody today?" Tom asked. "I see no books or other material from other classes."

"We stopped off at our rooms to unload," Frank answered for the group.

"We may not have books, Professor," Everett said, "but we are loaded for bear."

"Am I the target?" Tom asked.

"Not really," Jack answered. "I think we are after those Courtiers we were talking about yesterday."

"That is why we are here," Tom responded, as he took the offered position against the tree. "Finding them is not the problem. Understanding them is our task. Are we ready to begin the search?"

"We stopped off at the store and picked up a soda on the way over," Frank said. "Would you want one before we get started?"

"No. I had one about an hour ago. I'll hold off until we break for exercise or other needs. Thank you anyway, Frank.

"I noticed that there are four brands of soda among the six of you," Tom commented. "How so?"

"Different tastes, I guess," Sam answered.

"Maybe different personalities," Tom responded. "Our first target for discussion — personality."

"I thought we were going to talk about Courtiers?" Alec said.

"We are," Tom answered, "and they all have different personalities. No two of them are quite the same."

"From what was said yesterday," Frank said, "they all have the same target — to be needed."

"Are you needed, Frank," Tom asked. "How about the rest of you? Are you all agreed that you are needed?"

"You asked Frank if he was needed," Alec said, "and then you tell the rest of us that we are. You seem to have no question about the fact of our being needed."

"I don't," Tom answered. "My problem is to get you to agree."

"We seem to have difficulty," Alec said, "not in the area of our job title or our work but in this new concept of the courtier and his relationship to the Boss. To be needed by the Boss for some reason other than what we were hired for is not easily accepted."

"By your own admission, Alec, each of you has been of some service to the Boss. Each of you has been brought into contact with him and has sufficiently impressed him with your qualifications or you would not be here. Your personality has been the measuring stick by which choice was made for the granting of the time and expenses necessary to have you partake of this experience. Each of you has come here from large companies. Think back to the staff with which you have been working. Were not there others in your age group with equivalent time on the job who might have been chosen? Why you?"

"I don't know how the others feel," Alec responded, "but I had thought that my choice was due to the job I had been doing. I have worked hard over the last couple of years and made a name for myself with the accomplishments that resulted."

"Have not others done as well?" Tom asked.

"Possibly," Alec answered. "There are certainly enough people to choose from in our company."

"Take my word for a minute," Tom said, "that being productive, constructive, or imaginative on the job is not sufficient to attain advancement unless your method of presentation of your effort and the continual refinement of your relationship with all employees is also productive. People relationships are just as important as the effort of day-to-day labor. The people relationships that develop with superiors are most constructive. If not made, your efforts go unrewarded. Your work in your specialty will bring you to the attention of superiors. They will want to know you. They will initiate contact on some personal basis to get to know you. Personal relationships have the added effect of stimulating the effort in the specialty that you hold so dear. Recognition is stimulating medicine. We all need it and feed on it. When it is offered, it also gives to the Boss who offered it an opportunity to evaluate the recipient. He assures himself of continued effort and with personal contact learns of the potential of another member of his staff who may fit into his plans for the future. The personality of the employee under such scrutiny will determine to a great extent the future use of his talents. Is he to be locked up in some office or laboratory to continue his work or will he be brought out into the stream of activity within the company to grow with its progress? This evaluation is what our efforts here are all about. To me, it is not difficult to picture each of you under such evaluation. Obviously, each of you has done his job well, as it applies to the specialty for which you were hired. It is also evident that you have each attained some proficiency, by your personal approach to the system within which you are working, as it applies to people relationships.

"Your individual personalities have brought you to

the fore. You have been recognized for an asset beyond what you were hired for. It is this recognition that offers the reward, not the performance of the mechanical task that brought it to light. Can you all accept that distinction and admit its happening in your own personal situation?"

"There was no quick response from anyone. Sips of soda, lighting of cigarettes, and pulling up a fresh blade of grass to chew on, gave evidence of hesitation.

"You want us to admit that we are better than someone else in the office," Jack finally commented.

"Is that wrong?" Tom asked.

"I don't know," Jack answered, "but it sure shines a different light on what I have been doing over the last few years."

"I'll admit there are some duds in the office," Everett said. "Smart, for sure, as it applies to their knowledge of the job, but certainly not the type I would want to become personally involved with. I see what you are driving at, Professor, but I am not certain of how it applies to me."

"Do the rest of you feel the same way?" Tom asked.

"They did.

"Will you admit that you won?" Tom asked.

"I hadn't thought of it as winning," Sam said. "I'm not sure of who was in the race — if there was one."

"Were you the only person in the company who might have been chosen for the course?" Tom asked.

"Hell no," Sam responded, "there are dozens of guys my age who might have been in line for it."

"Then you did win?" Tom asked.

"In a sense, I guess you're right, but I hadn't thought of it that way. Are we all in the same boat?" Sam questioned.

"I don't like the boat analogy but you are all

winners or you wouldn't be here," Tom said. "and if you will look back on the scene from which you came to this course, you will see that it was a personality difference that made the winning possible.

"When I sat down here, I said we would take up the personality subject as our first effort today. We are already deeply into it. I sense that you can each admit winning your presence here through something other than the mechanical effort on the job. The simple reticence you show makes evident to me the strength of those personalities and the fruitfulness that they have already generated. In each of you, there is difference. That is due solely to the fact that you are human. We each have a uniqueness of personality. None of us attacks a problem in the same way. I don't want to get into a psychological discussion of personality, only discussion of how to improve the one you have. The presence you offer to the world is your greatest asset. Within the business community, that presence will determine your future."

"The presence you speak of, Professor," Tim said, "is this the same thing as the concept Courtier we were into yesterday?"

"Exactly, Tim. It stems from your personality and is the guiding force in making life on the job fruitful — beyond dollar reward for mechanical effort. It distinguishes you by your ability to fill needs other than your job classification specifications. It makes of you a more worthy tool. By so doing, it opens the doors to upward mobility that you so desire."

"This is why you called us Courtiers yesterday," Alec said. "Our presence on the job and the winning of the contest, as you call it, puts us in a class by ourselves. Is that it?"

"Yes, it is, Alec, and getting you to accept it has

not been easy. My judgment is that you have accepted it and now we can go on to the real purpose of the course — refining your qualifications."

"You want to improve our presence, as you put it," Frank said. "How do we approach that subject?"

"By simply asking ourselves, what makes for an acceptable presence," Tom replied. "There is no one sentence answer. The needs of the Courtier are myriad. He acquires them by study and awareness. The mastery of the art takes time. All we can do here is offer suggestions and review the various items that make up the Courtier's armament. Hopefully, back on the job, the rewards of our effort will show themselves by placing each of you in position to practice what we have discussed."

"Do you have a list of things that the Courtier needs?" Jack asked.

"In a sense we do, Jack," Tom answered. "I said we would start off our discussion today with personality. We have, but we have not yet considered differences in those personalities and how those differences can be used to advantage. The many items we will take under discussion must be considered in light of the individual personality of the one attempting to master them. Each will take a different path to mastery. This is the way it should be. As we consider the many items to be added together to attain professional status as Courtier, we must not forget that each will be handled differently and brought to fruition within the personality of the one developing the skill. Our discussion is basically about skills — knowing they exist, developing them, putting them to advantageous use.

"I told you yesterday, as you were leaving the classroom, that you might not like some of the things we were going to discuss. They are very personal. They are in a sense, the parts that make up the whole that is so important. They must be discussed openly, with honesty and straightforward commentary. You will find their presence or omission in many of your own co-workers. If honest, you will see their presence or omission in yourselves. We can start with a simple and readily understandable skill — manners."

"Oh, how my mother would like to be here," Tim said. "I haven't heard that word for over eight years. Since I left home, in fact."

"Apparently, she taught you a few," Tom responded. "I don't think they teach them in college."

"That is for sure," Frank said. "When you're educated, you are not supposed to need them. Not from what I see around the office."

"They went out with long hair and the freedom bit of the sixties," Jack commented. "Woman's Lib did away with a bunch. I doubt if they will ever come back."

"It depends where you're at," Alec offered. "They still apply in the Executive Suite."

"That, my dear Alec, is where we are," Tom responded. "Recognition. You see it and so do the others. Manners are demanded but not specified."

"And if you don't have them," Everett said, "you are not a Courtier. Is that your approach?"

"Exactly," Tom answered. "You are not worthy to be accepted into that environment."

"Makes sense," Jack commented. "I know how repulsive a few guys are in my outfit and I wish they would wake up to their problem. It makes for a tough association."

"There is a guy in my office," Jack said, "who drives all of us nuts. When he gets a cold, he brings in a pocketful of facial tissues. He uses them at the rate of one a minute and leaves the damned things everywhere. In your ashtray, on your desk, on his desk, in your car, on the table at lunch. He is disgusting. Manners — why hell, he doesn't know the meaning of the word."

"I swear," Alec said, "that most people were never taught table manners. There are a couple of guys in the office, in fact there is also a girl, that I just hate to go to lunch with. They eat like pigs. What is bothersome, is that you can't say anything to them about it. It is too embarrassing."

"How often do they get invited to lunch with the Boss?" Tom asked.

"We get the message, Professor," Everett said. "If this is the kind of thing the Courtier needs, well I must admit I can understand your definition. I can also verify your comment that the number of Courtiers in any organization is small. Manners are in short supply."

"What bothers me is the *why*," Jack commented.

"That is of no concern to us here, Jack," Tom said. "I understand your concern but there is little we can do to correct it, except by example. Times have changed in the last ten or more years and one loss has been the courtesy of man-to-man. Manners, the tool of such courtesy, have been set aside. Call it a sign of the times. Its general demise does not mean that it is no longer in vogue. As with so many things, it depends on who you select as associates. A safe bet, is that those who still have manners will demand them of others. To be without them, places you in jeopardy, if you have aspirations for ladder-climbing."

"Those kind don't get invited anywhere, unless it

is by one of their own kind," Everett said. "They have a lot of company, so they don't feel unwanted."

"Manners add more to their makeup than you would suspect," Tom commented. "Manners, as items, make for a manner in a person. It is this manner that is the essence of the Courtier. Where do such manners come from?"

"Most of it is just common sense," Frank offered.

"Much of it comes from the home of the person," Everett said. "The way they were brought up."

"Not necessarily," Frank responded. "I know guys from fine homes who act like jerks. They act like they just try to be repulsive. I don't think the home is the source. Not completely."

"Let's take an example," Tom said, "and we may get some idea of the source. How are you at introductions? You are standing in an office with five or six people, all high level people, and in walks a good friend whom you truly respect . . . and you are in the position of having to introduce him to the group. Can you handle it?"

"That is a task I dislike," Sam commented. "I always get flustered."

"I am always afraid I will forget a name," Everett said. "Sometimes I do and it is embarrassing."

"Names don't bother me," Alec said. "I always wonder if I should use titles. I usually don't because I'm afraid of getting one wrong."

"Your embarrassment and concern for doing the wrong thing is evidence of your awareness of the necessity of doing it right," Tom said. "Where did that awareness come from?"

"I can't say," Everett answered. "I have always known it, I guess."

"Certainly not always, Everett," Tom said. "Your

mother never taught it to you — I would suspect. You didn't get it from school. Is there a school of manners within your company? I doubt it. You picked it up on your own."

"What are you driving at, Professor?" Alec asked.

"Manners are mostly self-taught," Tom answered. "Once one is aware that manners are part of living, it is not difficult to attain a high level of proficiency by observation and study. The more proficient one becomes the more observant he is of the omission in someone else, and thus his own level continues to rise. Manners embrace a whole range of characteristics. Many are seldom considered. This is why I said earlier that manners make for a manner in a person. This manner reflects the awareness of many items, each classified as manners. Little things, like breaking into a conversation at the wrong time, walking into an office without just reason, picking up the phone when you know there is someone on the extension. The list is ever so long. There is no need to burden ourselves with examples. The idea is that we know they exist and we do our utmost to free ourselves of the infraction. It is not easy to find a book or set of instructions on manners. You can read the etiquette books but they give broad outlines. Manners and the use of them comes from constant awareness of doing what is right — watching others and when necessary, asking for help. This last gets difficult as finding someone to ask can be trying."

"I learned which fork to pick up by watching," Jack said. "I didn't get much in that area of training at home. No reflection on the family but there was just no need of it. We never had more than one anyway."

"It is always in the best of manners to wait or to

66

restrain yourself, Jack," Tom said. "From such restraint, much can be learned. The person who jumps into everything without thought of the consequences usually drowns. By use of restraint, you get to watch others. Not always fruitful, I grant you, but in association with those to whose level you aspire, it can be most rewarding."

"The consciousness of manners seems to come forth when you are in the company of certain people," Sam commented. "It is almost as if the ones you are with, having good manners, bring out the feeling to do likewise. On the other hand, if you are with people who care nothing about manners, you seem to fall into their attitude. Why is this?"

"It's just like swearing," Jack said. "In and around the plant, working with guys on the floor, swearing is the norm. Move into the executive office area and you tend to be more careful."

"Association has a great bearing on both," Tom said. "In either case, there is the feeling of need to gain recognition. The human tendency is to become like those we are attempting to influence. When with the crude, act crudely. When among the gracious, act graciously. This may seem logical in its consideration, but it is not the way of the Courtier."

"We must consider the objective," Tom continued. "The Courtier's prime purpose in life is to improve his total performance. He strives for the needed tools that will fulfill his objective. In practice, he cannot take the path of least demand at any time or he loses the edge. As he develops graciousness, he must practice it under *all* conditions."

"I would suspect he would lose many friends along the way," Frank commented. "Like Jack said, if you are among the plant people you tend to swear. If you take a holier than thou attitude among them, you would soon be an outsider."

"I'm not sure that is the case," Alec said. "I know a guy in the office who is always the gentleman. He is loved in the pressroom by all the workers. In fact, he gets more cooperation than others who are like the workers in their speech and actions. I have never heard him swear or say a bad thing about anyone. He fits in with the Boss and in fact is with him a great deal, both inside and outside of the office. He apparently sees no need to fall into the trap of changing his speech as he moves from one group to the next."

Graciousness is acceptable at all levels of human endeavor," Tom said. "What is not acceptable is a show of superiority. If one is tempted to show affectation among those he feels superior to, he will lose friends, as you suggested, Frank. We tend to think of swearing as a manly trait. The thought is wrong. There is no loss of manliness to any man who graciously practices the art of cultured speech. Any assumed loss of manliness is far outweighed by gained respect from a known content of learning and graciousness. A solid opinion of self, based on structured learning and offered to the world with grace, showing no evidence of self-praise or bragging, will be accepted with most rewarding results. The Courtiers must strive to attain such acceptance."

"Are you implying that rough-talking groups will aspire to a higher level of conversation if one in their midst has it?" Tim questioned.

"Not always, Tim," Tom answered.

"We do it, when the Boss walks into the room," Everett said. "I've seen it happen many times. It is done out of respect, I would think."

"I still can't swear in front of my Old Man," Alec

68

said.

"I read somewhere, years ago," Jack offered, "that one should always talk as if their mother was in the room."

"An excellent guideline," Tom said, "In our consideration, however, we must go beyond the use of distasteful language and embrace the total spectrum of conversation. As you progress in your search for upward mobility, you will encounter people who have broadened their knowledge and want association with others who can relate to it. Communication is truly the sustenance of life. Its mastery is your most substantial weapon. Improving its ability to perform as demanded, requires effort."

"Great talkers can be a pain in the ass," Sam commented.

"Great talkers," Jack said, "usually don't have a great deal to say. They just talk. Most groups, with time, will turn them off."

"Good conversation in any field or on any subject, taking place under any circumstances, derives from knowledge," Tom said. "not knowledge that is superficial but knowledge of substance. You will see among any group, the speaker who is in command has depth in his knowledge of the subject under consideration. People don't like the re-hashed. They enjoy additions to their own storehouse. If the one they are talking with can add to that storehouse, they will engage him in extended conversation. The asset of the Courtier then, is his knowledge. Certainly, he must have a sufficient command of the language to transmit that knowledge but the bedrock of his strength is the knowledge. He must continually work to enlarge the source."

"When you speak of knowledge, Professor," Frank

questioned, "I get the feeling that you are not talking about the knowledge of the field in which you specialize. You are referring to cultural improvement, are you not?"

"I am, Frank, and it is to this end that we are to direct our efforts. From the beginning of our discussion, I have emphasized the Courtier's needs as being over and above his mechanical expertise. Most assuredly, in the improvement of conversation it cannot come from that mechanical expertise, except in the arena where that expertise is practiced. Once outside of that arena, the source material must have greater scope. To this end the Courtier must direct his effort. The most constructive tool is obviously reading but there are other tools and they must be found and mastered."

"You speak of culture, Professor," Everett said. "Within the business community we seldom think in terms of culture. It is not part of our normal consideration. Learning is primarily directed to within the business community itself. Our reading is of business and its effect on society. There seems to be such a need for this knowledge that little time is allowed for cultural pursuits."

"What Everett says is true, Professor," Sam said. "To feel comfortable among our peers we must keep abreast of what the industry is about. Beyond the business, we must keep up with what the government is doing and be current on world affairs. Little time is left for cultural pursuits."

"I would answer that with aggravating certainty," Tom responded. "If you will be honest with yourselves, you will admit that you do not have control over your own time frame. Either that, or you do not have the driving force necessary to improve the cultural level you admit to being stuck with. Any improvement you desire is possible, but possible only if you are willing to give it the time you so dearly love for the more pleasurable tasks. If the attainment of culture is not a pleasant pursuit, and you must learn first to make it one, certainly you will not give it the priority it deserves."

"Should we attain culture for purposes of being good conversationalists at the expense of maintaining our expertise in our mechanical function, as you put it, Professor?" Alec asked.

"Under no condition, Alec," Tom answered. "Remember, that from the beginning of this discussion we have emphasized that the function of the Courtier is over and above his mechanical pursuit. His improvement, then, must come from time spent over and above what is needed to maintain his mechanical proficiency. It can in no way be allowed to suffer. What is demanded to improve his cultural level must be attained with *added* effort. Mastery of the Courtier's graces requires expenditure of much time and, if desired, time that must be taken from pleasurable pursuits. This being the case, what are labeled as pleasurable pursuits might have the wrong priority."

"If we don't see the potential for pleasure in the pursuit of what we have labeled the graces of the Courtier," Jack said, "then it is going to be difficult to attain them. There is little I detest more than having to study something that has no interest or pleasure attached to the learning."

"Very true, Jack," Tom responded. "I think we all feel the same. There is, however, a way around this dilemma. The first step is to consider the incentive. Admission of the need can offer an incentive. If one's desire for perfection as Courtier is sufficiently strong, the problem of lack of interest in a given subject can be overcome. There is a strange phenomenon in learning. A given subject can have no interest to a person for years. Suddenly, for a wide variety of reasons, he reads a book on the subject and the gained knowledge of the subject changes his attitude completely. In many cases, he will become involved to the point of attaining great proficiency in that subject, where at one time its understanding was of no interest. I am sure you have all had such an experience."

"I can relate well to that idea, Professor," Sam said. "When I was a kid, I was forced to take piano lessons. I hated the sound of a piano and the time I was forced to spend practicing. From the time I was about twelve until I got out of college, I never touched a key. About a year ago, I read the life of Bach. I started playing with the organ that was in the apartment of a friend. I was hooked. I bought my own organ and now spend hours at the keyboard."

"You acquired an understanding," Tom said. "From that acquistion came the value of the subject and it became interesting. Any other examples?"

"I guess my hobby of painting falls into that category of change of attitude," Jack offered. "I used to joke about the unintelligible appearance of surrealistic paintings. A couple of years ago, I met a girl who was nuts about anything surrealistic. We went to art galleries and she would explain to me what the painting was supposed to represent. She even bought me a starter set of oils. I got hooked. I still don't like the surrealistic approach but I do paint and respect those who practice the surrealistic. I certainly changed my attitude."

"In your case, Jack, and the one of Sam with the piano, a change in direction came about with understanding of the subject. To develop an interest in any subject only requires the effort necessary to gain a basic understanding of its content. Its merit then takes over and interest is aroused. A desire for knowledge will generate the curiosity to start a search. Once underway, even if not of great interest, an understanding of the subject will permit further reading or partaking. Should great interest not be developed, there will be sufficient learning acquired to make you conversant in the subject. This is the objective we are seeking, to expand the tools of the Courtier. He need not be expert in a subject or an art but he must be sufficiently conversant to enter into conversation with one who has a more active or current interest. This ability makes him a welcome companion."

"He is welcome," Alec said, "to feed the needs of someone else. Is that the need you keep talking about, Professor?"

"One of them, Alec, and one that is very important to our Courtier. To build a warehouse of knowledge of wide variety, embracing the arts, music, the classics, history, as well as less intellectual fare such as baseball, golf, tennis, riding, sailing and all other pursuits of sporting men, makes the Courtier the welcome guest or companion. Such is his strength."

"The conversational ability seems to be his greatest asset," Frank said."

Conversational ability alone is not adequate, Frank," Tom said. "Within that conversational ability there must always be substance. One of you mentioned earlier that a talker can be boring. Very true. To talk with superficial knowledge on any subject soon turns off the listeners. The Courtier will pursue his effort in a given subject to a point where he becomes well-versed and factual in his background, so that he can offer constructive or interesting substance to any conversation. He then truly becomes a welcome addition to any gathering."

"My God, Professor," Sam said, "what you are proposing is a lifetime of study of the arts, music, the classics, and all those other items you mentioned a minute ago. That becomes one hell of a task."

"Sam, just think of how far you have progressed without even being aware of the need. It is not difficult. Really, all it takes is the development of an active curiosity. Direct that curiosity to the subjects of value, not those of pleasurable immediate pursuits, and you are off and running."

"Which areas of study are most important, Professor?" Alec asked.

"Importance is not the word, Alec," Tom responded. "Helpful would be more expressive of the need. What you are seeking is a broad understanding of life and the people who live it. We spoke briefly of music and the arts — of sporting activities and other recreational pursuits. These are fine and should be made active tools of the Courtier. He must, however, probe deeper to gain an understanding of man and mankind. The past holds the most useful key. A study of history and the personalities that made it, or were outstanding in its formation, offers great understanding; in a broader sense, the study of the past. The warriors, the philosophers, the rulers — all can offer guidance. From the reading necessary to attain familiarity with the past will come guidance for the future. You all aspire to be leaders. You want to advance within your company to positions at or near the top. Leaders must have awareness of man and his shortcomings. To study the past offers sources for this awareness. You have a two-fold project in hand as you acquire the grace of the Courtier. You satisfy your Boss' need and build the foundation that will be necessary when you attain the level of accomplishment dreamed about in these early years."

"When we acquire all this extra curricular learning, Professor," Everett said, "we might become inflated. I have seen a few examples and they were disgusting."

"That is for sure," Jack said. "We have a guy in the Advertising Department who constantly refers to the Romans and Greeks. He has some parallel to refer to for every happening. It gets sickening. He has been nicknamed the Scholar."

"He is no Scholar," Tom responded. "Bore is a more appropriate term. To flaunt knowledge of any kind is not the way of the Courtier."

"There is a question here, Professor," Frank said, "that needs discussion. To broaden one's mind is great. I have no problem with the idea. To acquire a mass of learning about subjects that you will never use seems to me to be somewhat wasteful of time. For instance, if I spend time getting a good foundation in architecture, learn all the nomenclature, become proficient so I can identify the style of churches throughout the world, and by just looking at an old building can give you a rundown on its architectural history, what will such knowledge add to my being a Courtier?"

"Possibly the first thing to consider, Frank," Tom responded, "is that you have widened your working vocabulary. That alone is a definite plus. You have given to yourself a new way of looking at things. You will see more, as you look about you. The knowledge gained will feed many other facets of your storehouse of knowledge. Learning always meshes with prior knowledge and feeds what is forthcoming.

To yourself, you have added substance. You may not run into many people or cases where the specific knowledge of architecture will be demanded. It is, however, part of your storehouse and surprisingly it will come out in related matters that need clarification during a time of explanation. Such knowledge need not be flaunted. It is to be used. On occasion, you will run into someone who has also become interested in the subject and you will have a means of relating to that person in a way that no other subject may permit. On the other hand, the world in which we move on a day-to-day basis becomes aware of our particular interests and our familiarity with specific subject matter. We then become sources of information to others who have questions on the subject raised in conversation that they are unable to handle. This applies not only to your question of mastery of the field of architecture but the building of a working knowledge in any area of learning. There is never waste, as you put it, in spending time acquiring additional facts or a working knowledge of a new field of interest."

"But the average guy that we work with on a day-to-day basis normally doesn't have any interest in something like architecture," Frank persisted.

"Do you plan to spend the rest of your life with those average guys," Tom asked, "or do you have hope of moving into a more challenging area of association?"

"So all of this learning you speak of is for the future?" Frank said. "We should become intellectual Boy Scouts. Always prepared. Is that it?"

"In a sense, that is a good comparison," Tom answered. "The word 'boy,' however, doesn't fit. We are talking of the preparation of men. Men who can converse intelligently. Men who are comfortable in all surroundings — willing and able to offer interesting and constructive input to any conversation. Input that comes forth without affectation.

"To have this input accepted," Tom continued, "it must come forth in a manner that is natural. The Courtier speaks only of knowns. He will not speculate to attract attention. He speaks with abundant truth. His method of presentation is never grating. He has an ease of offering that commands attention. What he has to say can and will be accepted as truth. He generates from practice an air of pleasantness that holds attention. Having established a conversational ability that is natural and pleasant, based on sound understanding, he will be asked for opinion and commentary on many subjects and considered for membership in any group. He becomes a welcome asset."

"He makes himself needed," Alec commented. "Is that it?"

"Precisely," Tom said. "We have spoken of need by superiors. There is need of good conversationalists in all manner of circumstances. The Courtier fits. He is an asset to any gathering, in or out of the workplace. The conversational skills we are talking about are by no means limited to the workplace, although that is our prime concern in this course."

"We are not all talkers, Professor," Everett stated. "I know many people who just don't have a lot to say, anytime. They are basically quiet. Where do they fit, as Courtiers?"

"Courtiers are not talkers, Everett," Tom answered. "They will never utter a word that is unnecessary. Here lies the key. A quiet man is usually listened to when he does speak. Is that not true? Because he is quiet, there is about him an air of understanding. People listen when he has a word to offer. I do not feel that you should take the idea of being quiet though. What we are searching for is the mean. The middle ground. Conversation should come easily to the Courtier. He should have no difficulty in expressing himself clearly, without affectation, on any subject that arises. Certainly, his knowledge of the subject will determine his willingness to speak, but he is willing to speak and does so comfortably. He is neither quiet nor boistrous. But of profound importance, he must be listened to. This is the mark he seeks."

"Don't you see a conflict here, Professor," Sam asked, "with the personality of the individual? Everett mentioned the quiet guy who has little to say. What about the guy whose personality is such that he is a talker? Not one who is raspy or grating but just a good talker. Are we saying that he is out of luck as a Courtier?"

"Certainly not, Sam." Tom answered. "In reality, he has a distinct advantage. Conversation comes easy to him. He need only add knowledge to his ability to reach the goal of being listened to. Each has a different task ahead of him. The quiet man must be willing to attain a more relaxed attitude that permits more frequent offerings to a conversation, while the easy talker must work to restrain himself. It may not be restraint or relaxation that either need but a more comfortable awareness of self. The Courtier must gain confidence. He must feel confident with his ability. There is absolutely nothing wrong with self-confidence. It is a most necessary tool for success. Its control is the problem. We don't hear the word used much in our generation but the old concept of sageness offers us a wonderful framework to consider, as a target for our Courtier."

"Doesn't that word sage apply more to older people?" Tim asked.

"Not really, Tim," Tom answered. "Wisdom is attained not from years of living but from what has gone into the years that have been lived. Certainly, we think of a sage as an older person but the quality of sageness can be in man at any mature age. Wisdom is not limited to the old. History abounds with men who have attained it in their youth and utilized the attainment to wonderful ends. The mastery of acumen, judgment, and shrewdness may develop into sagacity but at the same time, if controlled, it can reflect the sage. He need not be one of long life but one of years that have been wisely utilized. We must keep in mind the ability of man to adjust to needs and circumstances. We have spoken of both, frequently. To attain the glory of the Courtier demands adjustment. Our purpose here is to make clear the value attached to the objective, and hopefully offer means of attainment."

"Professor, I am a journalist," Alec said. "Does any of this fit into writing or are you solely speaking of the spoken word?"

"Alec, our discussion is about communication. We loosely use the word *speak* too frequently. What we are really seeking in the Courtier is the ability to transmit ideas and do so in such a manner that a willingness on the part of the recipient to listen is assured. The written word is no less valuable than the spoken word. Each must be offered with similar quality. You certainly have been taught, and see clearly in your endeavor, the unpleasantness of either poor writing or writing that does not offer substance in its presentation. It should then follow, that mastery of the spoken word and the ability to communicate with comfort, ease, and a pleasant manner to people willing to listen, for the expected value of the offering, is no less important than the ability to act in a similar fashion when writing. All of the qualities we have listed as necessary for the Courtier in his conversational ability apply equally to the written word. In your case, Alec, you have by your mechanical expertise, a distinct advantage in written communication. Your task is one of increasing the total knowledge to feed the writing. For the rest of you, while you were acquiring your education in your specialty you did not receive excellent training in the mechanical aspect of the written word and you now have the added burden of improving that ability. Unfortunately, within the specialties that you have selected, especially in the sciences, there is not the emphasis on writing that at one time embraced all curricula. The art of writing demands of you who have majored in other fields a great deal of effort to polish it, whereby the Courtier may shine through. In Alec's case, he has a jump on you. His effort, then, will center on the spoken word."

"Should we take courses in writing?" Everett asked. "I'm one of those engineers who has one hell of a time writing anything other than a report. I think the last time I wrote an essay I was in high school."

"I see no reason to take courses," Tom answered. "You have each been through a school of higher learning and been taught the habit and practice of learning. If the mechanics of writing bother you, time with texts on grammar and prose should be sufficient."

"My Old Man was a writer," Alec offered, "and

he told me that to write a good letter, which I seem to feel is the chore of the Courtier, as it applies to writing, you should learn to write love letters. He explained it this way. Write a love letter that will fully satisfy the girl to whom it is addressed but make it of such content that you could read it to a bunch of guys and not get razzed."

"That is impossible," Tim said.

"Not really," Alec responded. "I have tried it many times and have come pretty close. It is good exercise — a damned good exercise."

"Your example has more substance to it, Alec, than you realize," Tom said. "The idea and the doing — the practice and the proficiency gained — are the true concept of what the Courtier must establish as his approach to all endeavors. The professionalism he seeks requires established targets and going about the work of attaining those targets with effort that will advance his cause. Your Old Man was a fine teacher. Apparently you listened to what he had to say — being a writer yourself."

"I will admit that I can write, Professor," Alec continued, "but when it comes to talking, I sure wouldn't want to have to speak lovingly to some gal in front of a bunch of guys. I'd feel like a jackass."

"You think you are alone?" Frank asked. "Hell, I freeze, if I have to talk to a group larger than we have right here. If there are women present, not gals my own age, but older women, I get so nervous I just keep quiet. You say we don't need writing courses, Professor, to polish our writing skills — how about speaking?"

"Courses in speaking are normally designed for the person who wishes to be more comfortable or effective on the rostrum," Tom answered, "This is not the platform of the Courtier. Nevertheless, a course in this manner of presentation can be helpful. If nothing more, it can reduce the level of hesitancy that we all have at times in confronting people. The mechanics of conversation must be gracious and if hesitancy is a factor in a person's personality, then I would recommend a speaking course. Beyond this one area of helpfulness, I see no value in such. Developing conversational ability can be more readily assisted by the acquisition of total knowledge. If we are knowledgable in a subject, it is not difficult to discuss that subject. Good conversation comes to the fore when the participants are knowledgable and interested. With these two conditions in place, hesitancy will normally be set aside. Refinement, at this point, comes from practice. Having frequent opportunity to expound with grace on a wide range of known subject matter will more quickly hone the edge of conversational ability than any course you may submit to."

"Having accepted the challenge of broadening our knowledge and honing our skills, as you put it, Professor," Sam said, "where do we get the opportunity to practice, that you say is so necessary? Among my peers there are few who will discuss subject matter of the type we have been listing."

"The opportunity to utilize the tools we are discussing, Sam, does not always present itself overnight. There is no happening, as you younger people use the term. The process is one of slow growth over years. The building of the storehouse of knowledge that we spoke of does not happen overnight, nor does the call to graceful conversation have any great degree of frequency early on. The process is gradual. Your increase in knowledge comes slowly, as do the opportunities to practice. What you must accept is the need for the training and the confidence demanded when called upon to practice it."

"Then the Boy Scout idea that Frank put forth a while back," Tim said, "does have some value. We must be prepared. We should be in shape to perform."

"I don't like the word 'perform' any more than I did the word 'boy,'" Tom said. "To be prepared is the right idea. Not, however, as a boy. The concept is fine, but be careful of the word. The arena into which the Courtier places himself is adult- orientated. There are no written rules. Acceptance within that arena can be most bountiful. Rejection from it can be brutal. It is not a place for boys. Men only will survive. As to performance, my reason for not liking the word is simple. It conveys the idea of acting. The Courtier cannot be an actor. his activity in any circumstance reflects a way of life. If it does not, his effort will be seen immediately as a charade, and he will be dismissed. A most disheartening setback, as he may never be offered another opportunity to recover. The Courtier develop slowly. The development is based, above all considerations, on truth — of which we will have more to say in the days to come."

"There has to be more to this development process of the Courtier than we have spoken of so far, Professor," Jack said. "It can't be all speaking and writing, frosted with a nice covering of manners."

"You are so right, Jack," Tom agreed. "But for today, and I see we have exceeded our allotted time, speaking and writing, and as you put it, the frosting of manners, will suffice. We'll meet in the classroom tomorrow, as I understand we have bad weather moving in tonight."

Tom stood up and like the others now standing, stretched, before starting his walk back to the building.

It was still quite warm and he would miss the pleasant shade of the oak and the relaxed atmosphere of this day tomorrow in the classroom. It had been a good session and he felt the class was accepting the idea of the Courtier.

"Professor, we will be stopping off for a beer on the way to our dorm," Tim said. "Would you care to join us?"

"Thank you, Tim but not today. I have a loving wife who is expecting guests this evening and I dare not upset her plans. Possibly next time, as I do enjoy the 'on tap' variety. I'll see you tomorrow."

He heard the word Courtier twice before the class walked out of hearing distance.

DAY THREE

THE IDEAL COURTIER

The Square was rain soaked, as Tom stood looking out of the window of his office. A good day to be secure in a classroom.

Specifics might not set as well as the generalities we talked of yesterday. Tom thought to himself. Certainly, there will be one or more who has his toes stepped on today. I do hope they have sufficient grasp of our objective to accept the possible criticism. We shall soon know.

He walked down the hall to the classroom and at five minutes before three, found them all in place. He noted, as he had in the past, that they were in the same seats they occupied two days earlier. Students seemed always to take the same seat, even if none had been assigned. He had wondered many times why.

"Good afternoon," he said, as he stepped behind the desk. "A nasty day."

"You would have been late for your party last night," Tim said, "if you had come along for a beer. We gave the Courtier a pretty good going over — until almost nine o'clock."

"There was no homework assignment," Tom said. "How come?"

"Just talking," Everett said. "We didn't identify many Courtiers among our fellow workers, Professor. Seems like you narrowed the field with yesterday's discussion."

"I told you yesterday," Tom responded, "that they were not great in numbers. It is a most difficult profession. We will narrow the potential even further today. We need to look at specifics and the doing may not suit your fancy. As Jack suggested yesterday, there is much more to the Courtier than the master of conversation with good manners. Before we get into that discussion, I would like to mention two thoughts on conversation and learning that we neglected yesterday.

"With regard to speaking and writing, there is need to develop a neatness of offering. To be listened to with assurance of effect, either through the spoken word or writing, it is necessary to develop a style that is straight-forward and free of embellishment. There is the need to reason well before initiating communication. It is in this regard that I made the issue yesterday of knowing yourself and your capabilities. It becomes necessary at times to look inward to determine the depth of knowledge in a subject before launching forward on a course that could turn rocky. Getting in over your head by offering general commentary can be unsettling. At times, you may feel that a word from you is expected. If you are not prepared for the offering, do not be tempted to get involved. Silence is a wonderful partner. If you feel some comment is demanded, fear not expressing lack of knowledge on the subject, for although you may feel inferior at the time, the respect gained will be substantial. Let others lead the way."

"Don't you get left out of the conversation if you take that approach, Professor?" Jack asked.

"Not at all, Jack," Tom answered. "You can question or add comment later that will keep you involved. With this approach you assure your companions of your honesty — a most worthy cause to admit of less than a professional opinion on some subject that you are obviously not equipped to pursue."

"It is embarrassing to comment on some subject and then find that there is an expert in the house," Sam said. "I have had the experience."

"Exactly what I am talking about, Sam," Tom said. "It can be a most unsettling experience.

"The second item I wanted to go over before we continue with today's schedule is the forced entry into conversation. Entry based on enthusiasm. A subject is broached or a question asked of something that you have abundant knowledge of and are well prepared to handle. To take the conversation and expound your knowledge is most tempting. The true Courtier will hesitate — restrain his enthusiasm. He will let someone else initiate the response and possibly get involved somewhat later — usually by being asked for his opinion. In the case in point, you might compare the suggestion to the Gospel example of taking the lower seat and waiting a call to a more favored position. The hesitation gives added plus to any offering, as introductions to the subject have been made and the path to constructive offering may well have been made clear."

"My God, Professor," Everett said, somewhat frustrated, "are you telling us that we have to be cautious under all circumstances when we are with people? Life would get rather uninteresting, wouldn't it?"

"Only if the caution is forced, Everett," Tom answered. "If the caution is habit, there is no loss of interest in life. You must remember, our total effort in this discussion of communication is to strive for an ability that commands respect. The items we are discussing will detract from respect and not further the cause of the Courtier."

"Must he always have a cause?" Alec asked.

"His cause is a way of life that will bear the fruit that he seeks," Tom answered. "He has no other objective. His commitment is total."

"We spoke yesterday about manners," Tom continued. "We also commented on the total manner of our Courtier. To develop that manner, that presence that makes for an outstanding Courtier, we must consider the specifics that add to that presence or detract from it. We need to list, if you will, the studies he must undertake to attain the knowledge that we have said is so necessary. We will also consider the many graces he must attain and the many unpleasant habits he must free himself of, if the manner he wishes to present is ideal.

"If he wishes to be an asset to those with whom he wishes to associate, his offering must be extensive. We spoke of music yesterday and to some extent, painting. An appreciation of both and some degree of ability in their practice is most necessary. He should attain such by something other than just reading. He needs performance if he is to be conversant to any degree of acceptability. He has to paint and he has to play. He needs understanding of oils and comfort with the terms of music. To get either, mastery of the brush and some proficiency on at least one instrument is essential. He need not become a virtuoso, yet without the physical contact his knowledge will be shallow. He will be wanting."

"Does this approach apply to everything?" Tim asked.

"It must, Tim, if the Courtier is to be complete," Tom answered. "Take some other examples. Golf, for instance. Can you talk a good golf game without having played a number of rounds? No. Comfort in the knowledge of golf comes from many hours on the course, also much discussion with others who have attained success or failure at approaching that golfer's ideal — par. With such experience, you can then feel the comfort that the doing has generated. Tennis would be no different."

"If the Courtier is to be complete, Professor," Sam said, "he is going to have to master one hell of a lot of activities. You are talking about a great deal of time, and more realistically a lot of dollars. What is on that list that you mentioned?"

"I'll throw the question back to you, Sam, and to the others," Tom answered. "What are the activities today among the top echelon people in your company? What sports, hobbies, entertainment, pastimes, recreational activities or cultural pursuits are most frequently discussed?"

"You are asking for the world, Professor," Alec commented. "The list is endless."

"So it may seem," Tom responded. "But again, as we commented yesterday, how far along are you with your present accomplishments? Certainly, you are not having to start from scratch."

"For starters, Professor," Alec said, "I have never

sailed a boat, ridden a horse, flown an airplane — three of the activities that my superiors take part in regularly. I can't afford a boat, a horse, or an airplane. Where does that leave me?"

"Number one, Alec, you can read. You can hire a horse. You can take a few flying lessons. You can finagle a few rides on someone's sailboat. It is not necessary to own a horse, a plane, or a sailboat to have the knowledge we are seeking for our Courtier. We haven't spoken of it yet, but ingenuity certainly must be a characteristic of a good Courtier. Develop it. Make friends with someone who has a boat. Find a girl who has a horse. Take a part-time job at the local airport. There are ways to attain what is desired, Alec, if the will is sufficiently strong."

"We may not like some of those activities, Professor," Tim said.

"Like is not the criteria of measurement, Tim," Tom answered. "Yesterday, someone said that there was nothing they liked less than to have to study a subject that they disliked. I said then, and I must reiterate now, that until you have a working knowledge of any of these activities, you cannot make a judgment of like or dislike. They have to be tried. In most cases, you will find that liking will be forthcoming to a sufficient degree to attain a measure of expertise — at least adequate to sustain a constructive conversation. It may also be, that liking will develop to a point where the activity will become one of your specialties. Neither will occur unless you initiate the pursuit. What we are seeing in this endeavor is the nurturing of the basic drive of curiosity. It should be your closest friend. Through it you will, with time, gather the knowledge you seek."

"How do you put priorities on these pursuits, Professor?" Everett asked. "Which one of the sports, for instance, should we tackle first?"

"I don't see where priority enters into the consideration at all, Everett. You are seeking a broad spectrum of awareness and familiarity with all activities. Why encumber the effort with priorities?"

"Well, if your boss is a real hot-shot golfer, wouldn't your first priority be to get into the game of golf?"

"In that context, yes. But by so doing, you should not neglect the other pursuits."

"In Alec's case," Tim said, "where his superiors were active in flying, sailing, and horseback riding, would not his priorities be established?"

"Only to the extent that his immediate effort should be in those particular pursuits. If he changed jobs, his objectives would change, at least on a short term basis. We are seeking to give the Courtier a full knowledge of completeness, as mentioned earlier. The immediacy of a given need is obvious. Attainment of completeness is not a short-term project. The process takes years. Don't forget that the sporting activities are only one facet of the objective. I will grant that in this age they are most necessary. Keep in mind, that while sailing, for instance, conversation is not limited to that activity. On any boat, much time is available for discussion and intellectual pursuits. With most sporting activities, conversation is not limited to the activity itself. It is by placing yourself in these particular circumstances that your broadness of base comes to the fore. It is just that circumstance that offers to the Courtier his greatest opportunity."

"You mentioned cultural pursuits, Professor," Jack said. "Which ones did you have in mind?"

"All of them, Jack. We spoke of music and painting.

Consider the value of the symphony, the opera, the theater, museums, study of the classics and history — the list is endless. Enough for a lifetime."

"That brings up a question, Professor," Alec said. "At what point is one sufficiently skilled to be called a Courtier?"

"At what point is one considered a Journalist, Alec?" Tom responded.

"I have the title with a couple of years experience. I was called a Journalist the first day on the job. My college training gave me the right to the title. The effort to attain it was in one subject. This Courtier bit seems to me to be too embracing to expect a title at my age or for many years to come."

"Age, with the Courtier, is no less a criteria than it is with the Journalist," Tom said. "Or for that matter, with any other title that attends a mechanical specialty — Chemist, Marketing Man, Advertising Executive, or Engineer. In my opinion, each of you commands the title Courtier. You have each attained a level of proficiency that has already presented reward for your effort. Granted, we have clarified the term Courtier for you and are seeking to give you what you may not have considered additional or necessary tools, but that does not detract from the fact that you have attained the title with your own awareness. Certainly, like a Journalist or any other on the job title, you will grow and enlarge your ability in that field. You will do likewise, as Courtiers."

"In my case, Professor," Jack said, "my present friends, either within the business world or outside of it, are not widely active in many of the things we have discussed. It will not be easy to get involved in some of the sports or other pursuits you insist are necessary for the Courtier's development. The others must have the same problem. How do we handle it?"

"A fair question, Jack. Contrary to the attitude that I would assume each of you have, friendships are restraints. They have value, no question. I would not under any conditions suggest that they not be made or that any in place should be broken. I would ask that you look at them in relation to what your objectives are in that system within which you are working. Are they helpful?"

"You don't make friendships for their help," Sam said.

"If you have a friend that cannot associate with a group who you wish to become involved with," Tom responded, "do you take him along?"

"I don't follow your question," Sam answered.

"You have developed a friendship with some associate in the company or from early college days. You enjoy his company in certain sports or social activities. You move into a new group of associates who are of a different nature and have interests in the arts and music, for instance. Your old friend has no interest or even dislikes music and the artistic pleasures of life. Do you insist he join you with the new group or do you go alone, knowing that he would be out of place?"

"I wouldn't want to embarrass him," Sam said. "I would most likely just go and not ask him."

"Fine," Tom said. "You are moving out of his realm of likes and dislikes, are you not?"

"In a sense, yes," Sam answered, "but that doesn't mean I drop him as a friend."

"No, but it does mean that he cannot be of help to you in your new interest — right?"

"I never thought of it that way," Sam responded.

"If the new interest is sufficiently satisfying, you

will spend a great deal of time with it. The doing will draw you into other pursuits, again that may not have interest to your old friend. You see him less frequently and with time the friendship diminishes in fervor and he becomes one you see only on rare occasions. I am certain each of you can recall an example of what I just described. Now, why did you move away from his association and get involved in something that was alien to his likes? It was most certainly to be of pleasure to yourself. The new associates aided you in attaining that pleasure. They became helpful."

"That is a damned cold way of looking at friendship, Professor," Everett commented.

"It may seem so at the time, Everett, but as you move on in life, you will see that those you are in most cases calling friends are more realistically associates. Most of us develop very few true friends during life. Only a few friends survive our change and theirs in likes and dislikes. We like to be together solely as human beings, not just to enjoy some outside activity. This kind of relationship will last and usually last for a lifetime. The quick friends on the other hand, more rightly called associates, fit an immediate need. They join you in some pleasurable, or from the Courtier's viewpoint, constructive pursuit. They are the friends, as you will call them, who assist you in the acquisition of the knowledge you are seeking. They are helpful. You will use them until your interest changes or you feel you have received sufficient input from the current pursuit and move on to another — with a different group of friends."

"You are expecting us to make a hell of a lot of friends over the coming years," Frank said.

"Again, Frank, distinguish between friends and associates," Tom reminded him. "If you are to broaden your interests with the clean-cut idea of furthering your own objective of making yourself more a needed and acceptable commodity in the upper strata of the business world, you are going to have to expand your associations to permit the learning process to proceed. This means moving out of your present circle of friends or associates. And, keep in mind, the process will continue as you move up through the system."

"What happens to all the old friends?" Alec asked.

"The old associates will fall by the wayside, as it were," Tom answered. "The few old friends will always be around, when you need them to cry on."

"You want us to use people?" Jack asked.

"Is there a more worthy cause?" Tom answered.

"You want us to admit that we have been doing this sort of thing right along," Everett said. "Doing it, as you say, without a cause. Is having a cause so critical?"

"Therein lies the strength of the Courtier," Tom answered. "To ramble through a life in the business community without a cause, places you among those you so clearly labeled Flunkies. They bumble, stumble, and move about with an attitude of self-importance that turns off the world in which they attempt to function. They develop no professional presentation of their gained assets. They force themselves on the scene, rather than being asked. A most profound difference. They are seldom welcome and always a burden. Should there be growth in their acquisition of knowledge, it is wasted."

"We are back to that concept of being needed, Professor," Alec said "Only this time you are saying that we are to design a broad based curriculum of focused self-improvement. Am I right?"

"Absolutely, Alec. We have discussed the need for broadening the base of knowledge. To do so is necessary, but to do so without objective leads to naught. The opportunity to utilize the gained knowledge will be elusive, if the presentation of the commodity is unpleasant. It is to this end that we now move. The Courtier, aware of the need for quality in presentation, observes the difficulties in the incompetent and strives to make his own presentation desirable."

"By not practicing the habits that make the so called incompetent unwelcome — is that it?" Jack asked.

"In a sense, yes, Jack, but I prefer to take the positive approach, rather than to look at the negative, and avoid it. The result will be worthy of the Courtier.

"As a professional, the Courtier presents an aura of confidence. He need not perform with affectation. His actions and speech present to the world assurance. He neither brags of his capability nor forces his knowledge upon his fellow man. He rests confident in the assurance that when called upon he will perform with grace. He offers no flattery, nor shows any great desire to win when placed in competition. His performance will be adequate; thus he competes with an air of enjoyment, certain that he can perform with excellence. Win or lose, he has exhibited a knowledge of the activity and given constructive offering to those who joined him in the doing. If he is superior in an endeavor, he wins. He will not diminish his presentation to foster pride in another. Nor will he irritate by boasting of his proficiency. He approaches all endeavors with nonchalance — sufficient in the knowledge of his own ability."

"Is he not apt to become a snob?" Sam asked.

"Not if in the design of his approach to the world, he uses caution. What will shine forth is grace, not snobbery."

"You just said that when he plays, he wins, if he has the capability," Tim said. "Does he beat the hell out of his Boss in a golf game? I would think that would be committing suicide."

"Not really. The Boss will know before the game, what he is to expect. If a Courtier is good, he should perform accordingly. To win is by no means detrimental. To win and rub someone's nose in the result is catastrophic. Realistically, if the Boss is a good golfer he will enjoy playing with a good golfer. If he is a hacker, he might improve his game if the partner, in this case the Courtier, gracefully offers assistance and doesn't brag about his own game. Here, we see the honesty that must be of paramount importance to the Courtier. It would be destructive to enter into dishonest performance."

"Suppose our Courtier is good but the Boss still beats him," Everett asked.

"The perfect result, Everett. Not always possible, but the advantage to be gained is most worthy. His quality is assured. His enjoyment of the game evident. He will certainly again be given the opportunity to challenge his partner and winning then becomes no detriment."

"This guy has to be crazy," Frank commented. "He plays the odds against the risk."

"Yes, Frank the Courtier is a gambler. A gambler in the truest sense of the word. He never bets on anything unless the odds are in his favor."

"You are assuming, Professor, that the Courtier is good at what he is doing," Sam said. "He had to start someplace and when he did he was not so good.

How does he handle this situation?"

"A fine point, Sam," Tom said. "In the early stages of learning, the Courtier will refrain from displaying his lack of ability. He will study or practice alone, or away from the center of prominence. He will admit to no knowledge or proficiency until he has satisfied himself that he can perform with assurance."

"A sneaky bastard, isn't he?" Alec said.

"Not really," Tom responded. "He knows that a less than quality performance could be detrimental to his cause. He has no intention of making himself the butt of any joke, nor the subject of detrimental commentary. He is building an image and there is no excuse for a performance that is less than constructive. It is to his distinct advantage to refuse participation either in conversation or activity, if he feels deficient. Avoiding what you are ignorant of is always excellent insurance. Never can an inept performance be justified."

"Can such perfection be attained, Professor?" Alec asked.

"Like in so many other things, Alec, perfection is relative. It is also, seldom attainable. The object here, as we define Courtier, is the seeking of perfection — reaching for its attainment. The desire to better a position — always striving. In a sense, to keep ahead of the pack. The problem is that the pack changes as the Courtier moves up through the system. His effort cannot be diminished at any stage of upward movement as new challenges are constantly being presented. As was said earlier, the development of the Courtier is a lifetime endeavor. The good Courtier is never satisfied. He continually hones the edges of his weaponry — always prepared for the next challenge. His confidence lends trust in his own judgment and with observed omission in any facet of his armor, he works diligently to fill the void. His curiosity is endless. The perfection you questioned, Alec, is continually sought."

"Does this guy trust anybody?" Tim asked. "It would seem that he would have to be a loner."

"The idea of trust is deadly, Tim," Tom answered. "Really, trust can only reside in yourself. If it is permitted to rest on another, your own position is placed in jeopardy. It is for this reason that self-confidence is so vitally important and it will arise only from diligence in the pursuit of knowledge. As to being a loner, as you put it, that is not necessarily the case. Being reserved and continually aware of the need for quality of presentation does not mean you have to be a loner. On the contrary, the Courtier is normally front and center in any gathering. Not by forced entry but by obvious need. His quality gives him the edge and his performance warrants the presence."

"Do you class him as an entertainer?" Frank asked.

"Not really," Tom answered. "Not in the sense of one who jests or tells stories. His input is always constructive. There is nothing constructive about a story-teller, especially one who has a bag full of the off-color variety. The Courtier is never the Jester. If he has the ability to cause laughter, it is done through tales of grace, not offerings of funny or risque' stories. Input of this type to any gathering is trifling in nature and adds nothing of substance. The one who offers trifles, ceases to be welcome. Whatever laughter may come from such an offering is soon forgotten. Entertainment of the variety you have in mind, Frank, is not of the Courtier's makeup."

"Does he laugh at other's jokes?" Jack asked.

"Laughter is a strange phenomenon, Jack. To laugh easily, as many do, is all affectation. Generally false, and seen as such by those who observe. It is not a plus. The courtesy of a smile is always necessary, in the case in point, but the hearty laugh is not demanded nor appropriate. In a general sense, laughter is a dangerous activity. If unbridled, it arouses emotion, a most uncontrollable enemy. When emotion enters upon the scene, the training of the Courtier is placed in jeopardy. He cannot permit such to happen. He must then, control his laughter. Years ago, the Jester was considered by many to be an enemy, for this very reason. "

"Is this guy ever going to have any fun?" Sam asked. "It seems that every attribute we ascribe to him detracts from his personality."

"Personality, only in the sense of 'Good Time Charley,' " Tom responded. "*That* he is not attempting to be. Personality has many faces, Sam. The one we want on the Courtier is by far the most difficult to attain. You must keep in mind that his natural personality will dominate his presence. What we are aiming for is the polish that will make him acceptable in all circumstances. We wish to take out the bad habits acquired and replace them with constructive alternates . . . alternates that will make of the natural personality a most worthy presence.

"The Courtier must be aware of traits in others that are not pleasant, or at the very least, cause discomfort. With honest self-appraisal, seeing any sign of similar characteristics in his own personality, he should work to remove them. In their place he must develop a plus. With each adjustment there arrives improvement. For example, he has a co-worker who is doing an excellent job. The guy knows it and never ceases to brag about his performance. The Courtier feels the needling, as do other workers, but the Courtier resolves that when his time comes to be overly proud of his performance, he will refrain from such boasting, as he sees its effect and the degree of destruction it can have upon the furtherance of his career. He learns from others' mistakes. He has the strength to admit a shortcoming and perseverance to overcome it. He is constantly re-appraising himself. The self-analysis he does on a continuing basis is his guarantee of growth."

"Can the guy ever relax?"

"He is always relaxed," Tom answered. "It would be impossible to be observant, as he must be, if he were not relaxed. We mentioned the characteristic of nonchalance. Acquired though it may be, it offers the relaxation necessary to learn. The high pressure personality makes mistakes. He breaks into conversation. He demands attention. He irritates. With his mouth always open, he can accept little in the way of input. He may temporarily domineer but will eventually fall into isolation. His desire for recognition is his undoing. The Courtier never seeks recognition. He never misses an opportunity to praise others, if they are worthy. He is most gracious in his appreciation of the attributes of others. Never does he boast of his own. If his worth is justified, he can live by that parable we spoke of earlier. He resides in the lower place, confidently aware that he will be called upward."

"We are back to the Boy Scout ideal again," Alec said. "Always prepared. You are painting a tough portrait for anyone to aspire to, Professor. This Courtier has to be one hell of a package."

"He is one hell of a package, Alec," Tom said.

"That is why he is needed."

"He may be seen as needed by those above him, Professor," Frank said, "but what about his peers? Will they not be turned off by him? Is he not apt to become the unwanted among his own co-workers, or his own age group, for that matter?"

"Not if he masters the art of knowing where he is at all times. He must adjust his presentation as needed. Certainly, he will not behave in front of his friends or associates on the ballfield, in a manner similar to that proscribed by temporary membership in a foursome on a golf course, where the President is footing the bill. Nor will he act the same with girls on a beach as he would on the deck of his Boss' yacht, where the Boss' wife and other ladies are present. His valor is dictated by discretion."

"You mean he is a chameleon?" Alec said.

"Not in the manner of quality of his presence — only in the openness with which he dares expose himself to criticism," Tom responded. "He must learn, that as he moves upward in his association with people he intends to capture, his potential for error is greatly increased."

"You mean he has enemies?" Everett asked.

"Yes, he has enemies. And their number will grow as he does. It will become fashionable to try to trip him. Many will try. He must be on guard. You asked if he were a loner. Well, as he succeeds in his efforts he is bound to alienate many of his associates. There will always be those who would relish his stumbling. As he progresses, it will be less tempting for him t become friendly with others. Friendly in the sense of openness in ideas and personal likes and dislikes. He must become reserved to a degree sufficient to protect himself. This should not alienate him from any of his peers. To them, he will appear mature and from the impression he will gain stature."

"How does he handle enemies, Professor?" Tim asked. "The ones who truly desire his fall from grace."

"We have to be cautious with the use of the phrase, Tim," Tom answered. "The enemies we speak of are not enemies by dictionary definition. They are not out to destroy by overt act. There are always the exceptions, such as the one who by uncontrolled vindictiveness seeks to plant seeds of distrust or by some means attempts to discredit him, but these are rare. The enemies we speak of in a broad sense are the many associates who see the Courtier advancing and dislike either his methods or his success. They take no overt action to impede but nevertheless, miss not an opportunity to demean or criticize. They may simply be jealous. To these, if they are of value to the Courtier, he will find some way of improving his association with them. In no case will he taunt them with his success. If he feels they are worthy of his effort, he will find a way to gain their favor by joining them in their activity or inviting them to join him. A better understanding of a person can in most cases raise the respect level felt for that person. Designed effort can make this possible.

"The Courtier cannot spend a great deal of time in this effort of reconciliation. He makes the effort only if the adversary is of sufficient worth to justify the time. He will, throughout his career, alienate many of his co-workers. He sees it happen and accepts the loss, knowing the good that has caused it is of greater value than the loss. In making this type of judgment, you may feel that he is cold in his approach to humanity. This is not really the case. More accurately, he is realistic. He feels the loss of friendship and it deeply affects him. He knows, however, that it is par for the course he is on and accepts the loss as the lesser of evils. His objective, or as we called it earlier, his cause, is too important to be inhibited by the loss of a few associates along the way. Such is to be expected. I don't feel that they can be classified as enemies."

"The true enemy — the one who uses the overt act to destroy — how is he handled?" Jack asked.

"The only defense against such a character, Jack, is the firm establishment of credibility. The stature of the Courtier must be so firmly established that attacks of this nature are seen so clearly by those in position to make judgments, that they are set aside, with the awareness of their crudity. Occasionally, they will be successful . . . and destructive. When this occurs, the true Courtier will write off the happening and avoid vindictiveness, instead devoting his time to re-establishing credibility. Every life has setbacks. They must not, however, be accepted as destructive — only as delays. The true worth of the Courtier will overcome such happenings."

"Your confidence level regarding this Courtier is amazing, Professor," Alec said. "I would think that if a person were knocked down by what you just described as happening at the hands of an enemy, the guy would have to up and leave. His position would be compromised. His feeling would be one of embarrassment, that could not be overcome."

"There should be no embarrassment, Alec, embarrassment comes from error. If there were no error, our Courtier need have no reason to depart or even regress. He knows the truth of the matter and his self-confidence will stand him in good stead. He stands tall and lets continued performance re-establish his credibility. There is no reason to run."

"On the flip side of this consideration of enemy, Professor," Frank said, "I can see our Courtier becoming the enemy. If, through his efforts and success he attains some degree of credibility, as you phrase it, with members of the staff or becomes a member himself, he will then be in a position to offer commentary and even judgment on those beneath him in the organization. He gains the power to destroy. Is he not then, an enemy?"

"You are jumping the gun on me, Frank . . . at that point in the Courtier's career, he is in the position where he can advise. We will get into that area of effectiveness, in detail, later this week. For now, suffice it to say that at that point of development in his career, his judgment would be based on what was good for the organization. If the good of the organization is the criterion, the word enemy does not exist.

"For today, let us stay with the formative development of the Courtier. The development of his manner has been central to our consideration. He presents a picture that reflects ease of doing. Nothing in his demeanor shows strain. He is aware that to stoop to the level of such things as foolish pranks or boisterous behavior will miscast his image. If these activities were at one time part of his makeup, he dare not revert. His growth must be seen, as his acceptance is realized."

"You seem to feel that he is always being watched," Everett said. "Is that normal? Do upper management people spend much time watching those beneath them?"

"They had better," Tom answered. "How else can they build a successful organization if they do not know the quality of their personnel? Every employee is under scrutiny. Once an employee is singled out for his unique quality, he is more closely observed. As our Courtier develops, he is by simple deduction a more valued employee. It is with this awareness, on his part, that he controls his demeanor. He knows he is under scrutiny and conducts himself accordingly."

"If you have to watch every action, evaluate each activity, and use caution in everything you say," Sam asked, "are you not apt to become so serious that you have no personality?"

"I don't feel that anything like that will occur, Sam," Tom answered. "By his very nature, the Courtier is straightforward. He has by acquisition of knowledge gained confidence. His awareness of his actions has become or will become, with practice, second nature. His caution, when caution is called for, need not in any way inhibit his relaxed presence. He instinctively knows when to speak and act and does so in a manner that is gracious. He has no fear. His greatest asset is that he is under control. His caution is by design.

"In his approach to any activity he does not jump in but uses restraint. You have an expression today that is very appropriate — 'Come on strong.' This is not the way of the Courtier. He will approach any situation with caution, be it verbal encounter or physical activity. By so doing, he lessens the danger of poor judgment. He is observant and will honor the opinion of others, if such opinion is constructive. He knows the value of experience and misses not an opportunity to be with those who have it. To associate with others experienced in an art or activity that he desires to master is his greatest teacher. He knows the value of age and does not shy away from the elderly. Acceptance of the fact that others have the learning he seeks draws him to age groups that the non-Courtiers avoid. He has no hangups about a so-called generation gap."

"We are back to the idea of the Courtier using people," Frank said. "You now have him using older people to further his cause. Has he no scruples?"

"I don't see where garnering education has anything to do with scruples," Tom responded. "You have come to me for education. You went to college and studied under many professors that were much older than you. Your own father had much to do with your education. If our Courtier is adept enough to see the value of learning from people older than himself, why accuse him of lack of scruples? Those with learning in any subject are most gracious about passing it on. In reality, they have difficulty finding students to train. Ego seems to get in the way. Our Courtier does not let his ego inhibit his progress. If he has ego, it will certainly not show. Thus, his grace."

"Will this grace he develops overcome the envy among his peers?" Tim asked. "I would think, that if you don't hate a guy like this Courtier, you would certainly envy him. How does he handle this situation?"

"Envy is not something that the Courtier seeks," Tom answered. "In fact, he works to allay it. He can do so by making light of any accomplishment. Where he sees the signs of envy, he will go out of his way to refresh the bearer's mind with input that will balance the deficiency that fosters the envious impression. It is not the Courtier's objective to foster ill feeling of any kind. Envy falls into this category, and it must be overcome. For the Courtier to be successful in fulfillment of his cause, he must be at peace with the world. His conflicts are with his own shortcomings, which he is working diligently to overcome. He does not need the added burden of disheartened peers."

"You paint him with a saintly countenance, Professor," Everett said. "I wonder if he really has it or is the countenance like the rest of his acquired learning — designed for effect?"

"The honesty that lies within the man will make that determination, Everett. Most things have the potential for turning sour. To carry the title Courtier with honor would make your implication an unlikely possibility."

"We have stressed the demeanor of the Courtier," Tom continued. "We have spoken of his presence and his manner. We must consider what to you is a most unlikely demand — his appearance."

"You mean we are going to dress him?" Alec asked.

"You're not going to tell us he wears a chastity belt," Sam said with a little uncertainty.

"No, and his personal habits are not our concern," Tom responded. "I would, however, suspect that one with the attributes of our Courtier would have difficulty keeping on a chastity belt. The presence we have given him will make him most desirable to the opposite sex — possibly to the point of tearing off such a device, if he were disposed to wear one."

"A plus I had not thought of, Professor," Frank said, "You know, I think I might like this guy after all."

"There is a good point in your response, Frank, and I think we should consider it here, as it has much to do with the Courtier's total manner. The word 'like' you just used — is it appropriate? Is the courtier's objective to be liked? I think not. What he seeks is respect, that feeling of deference, honor, esteem, that is awarded for worthy performance. He can have or acquire in his personality a likable trait, and certainly it would be a plus. He is not, however, in a personality contest."

"I don't see how he could function if he were not liked, Professor. All of this study we have discussed — would it not be wasted if he were an unlikable sort?" Alec asked.

"Certainly, if he was unpleasant, he could not function," Tom said. "It is difficult, however, to envision someone making the effort we have outlined — gaining the storehouse of knowledge we have considered — and still being unpleasant or in any way unlikable. He would certainly be aware of the need to be acceptable and, as such, a likable personality is demanded. What I am driving at is not so much his ability through personality to be liked but his need to be respected. This is of far greater value. In the development of his skills and the attainment of professionalism in utilizing them, his reward must be the respect of all with whom he comes in contact. If it not be, his effort will be wasted. The Courtier must reflect some degree of dominance among his associates. Not a dominance that is forced but a dominance that places him just beyond the edge of the common. From such a perch he is bound to acquire respect. If he is liked, as you said, Frank, this is a plus that can be most worthy. He must be able to function easily in both the world of his peers and the world to which he aspires. This borderline or ever changing position demands a respected presence in either. Now, whether you like him or not is not his concern. What he is concerned with is whether he has your respect. A subtle difference, possibly, but one that we must keep in mind."

"I don't see it as being subtle, Professor," Alec

said. "We have an editor at the paper who is the most unpleasant character you would ever want to meet, yet he is the most highly respected editor in the business. Certainly, he is no Courtier, but the distinction you are trying to make is not that difficult to understand."

"The difference I see with that editor, Alec, is that you are contrasting his personality with his mechanical ability. Keep in mind that our structuring of the Courtier is based solely on his non-mechanical qualifications. It *does* make a difference."

"Let's get on with this clothing idea, Professor," Jack said. "I am anxious to see how we dress our Courtier."

"We don't intend to dress him, Jack," Tom responded. "What we would like to do is consider his presence and determine what approach he should take in making it comfortable by his choice in attire."

"I don't get this word comfortable as being associated with dress, Professor," Sam said, "Comfortable clothing is not always the best choice in the business world."

"We are not talking about his comfort, Sam," Tom answered. "We are concerned only with the comfort he gives to others by his presence. And believe me, his clothing has a measurable bearing on the result."

"How do his clothes make others comfortable?" Everett asked. "That seems to be a strange comment, Professor."

"Not really, Everett. Let's take a couple of examples. How would you feel about having a tennis partner who showed up on the court dressed in dark brown slacks, black shoes, and a wild polka dot shirt?"

"He would be laughed off the court," Everett answered. "He would look ridiculous."

"Exactly," Tom said. "He would be out of place. All attention on the court and around the club would be focused on his attire — would it not?"

"He would be the center of attraction — that is for sure," Everett answered.

"Now, take another case," Tom said. "You make plans to have dinner at a fine restaurant early in the evening, before taking in a play at the theater. Four couples are involved. One of the men shows up in a sport shirt and slacks and the rest are attired with shirts, ties, and jackets. Who is uncomfortable?"

"O.K..." Everett said. "I get the word comfortable but those are ridiculous cases."

"Only insofar that they make the point," Tom said. "We must clearly understand the meaning of comfort, as it applies to dress. There is no question in the cases used. We are after a more subtle distinction.

"Today dress codes as we knew them for many years, have changed. Our relaxed lifestyle has permitted the easing of what once was a strict standard of dress. Yet, in many circles, the codes still retain a measure of conformity. In a general sense, being aware of where one is, has more bearing on selection of attire than it did in the past. Habits are easily formed, whereby the relaxed dress standard will establish a feeling of acceptance that can preclude consideration of formal attire as a need. A dangerous pit for any potential Courtier to fall into."

"Are you suggesting that our less formal clothing habits of today are wrong?" Frank asked.

"Not at all," Tom answered. I personally think they are great. We have a much wider selection of attire today than we ever had in the past. From the economic standpoint, it offers a plus in that the relaxed style is less costly. Have you priced a custom tailored suit

111

recently?"

"I don't own a suit," Alec said, "never mind a custom tailored one."

"But you will," Tom said, "and there will be times when you will feel comfortable in it, and by so doing make others comfortable as well."

"I'm still not clear on this comfort of others, Professor," Tim said. "I see the problem in the ridiculous cases you used but in day-to-day reasonable dress, where does comfort come in?"

"Clothing can be distracting, Tim. The wrong clothes attract attention. The Courtier has no desire to call attention to his presence. He need not be singled out by gaudy shirt, tie, pair of slacks, or a brilliantly colored sport coat. He is without exception the most conservatively dressed member of any gathering. His presence is assured by his manner and the constructive nature of his offering. He needs no sign to call attention to that presence."

"You figure that gaudy shirts are a bad sign?" Alec asked.

"On a beach in Hawaii, no. At a gathering after a golf game in a country club, they certainly would be. Only because it would call attention to the wearer and most likely generate some comment. The Courtier does not desire such comment, as it calls attention to his presence. It is not his way of gaining recognition."

"Would he wear a gaudy shirt on the beach in Hawaii?" Frank asked.

"He would have little choice, Frank." Tom answered. "If everybody on the beach had on a gaudy shirt and he showed up in a solid colored shirt, he would be out of place and would be calling attention to himself."

"Then you're not saying you have anything against gaudy shirts," Jack said. "The question lies with *when* to wear one."

"Exactly," Tom said, "and the same logic follows with every item of attire. To know when to wear a gaudy shirt is no less important than to know what color shoes to wear with each color of suit or slacks; also, to know how to select ties to complement a suit or to select sportswear appropriate in both color and style to fit any occasion. To be appropriately dressed is what is paramount. To be dressed with a measure of reserve reflects an awareness of the comfort of others and the ability to assure that comfort is not disturbed."

"This Courtier of ours is going to miss a lot of fun in selecting and wearing clothes, Professor." Alec said.

"Not really, Alec," Tom said. "When he ventures out to buy clothing, he has the pleasure of knowing that his choices are to be pluses in his effort to attain the professional status that he seeks. His objective has greater depth. He is not buying a piece of clothing with the thought that it will look great on him and will make others envious. If you recall, we spoke of envy earlier. The Courtier's objective is to be assured of his own correctness in choice of an appropriate item and to be certain that it does not call attention to its presence. He has no need of ego building. He is confident and secure in his own capabilities and need not use clothing for such a purpose. There is in the wearing of gaudy clothes the image of the Jester. We spoke of this subject earlier. Clothes complement the man and he will not jeopardize efforts in any area of performance by letting his attire reflect an image contrary to his objective."

"He is never gross. Is that what you mean?" Sam asked.

"In the sense of the word as used today, you are right. I would consider it a negative word, as it applies to our Courtier. It is more constructive to give him a positive word in the case in point — 'grace' for instance. He is ever graceful, and in the being he lends that comfort to others that we explained earlier as being so necessary."

"Where does he learn of all the needs of clothing with the wide range of his activities?" Everett asked. "These subtleties you speak of, Professor, are not normally written up by the clothing suppliers. Where does he get the information necessary to make such judgments?"

"Mostly, from his own awareness, Everett," Tom answered. "As with so many of the traits he acquires, he gained knowledge of right and wrong from observing others and noted in their actions the habits that were improper. It is the same with clothing. To know what to wear at a tennis match, he must take part in the game — observing and adjusting until his satisfaction with his own appearance is right. His strength comes from this ability to adjust — and we have spoken of this ability to adjust in regard to many of his objectives."

"We must keep in mind," Tom continued, "that we are talking about membership in the world of business. Certainly, our Courtier will be active outside of this world but his prime effort is directed at the success possible within this community. We tend to stray by putting him into other environments. It is to his credit that by attaining the tools necessary to perform in a professional manner in the business community that he will also perform adequately in any environment.

He is a total entity. He is not fractured by performing with one set of standards on the job and another when away from it. He is developing a life style and the sum of its parts reflect the image he presents. All of the qualities we have ascribed to him must meld."

"Do you carry this total presence idea to the extreme by suggesting he adjust his physical characteristics, Professor?" Tim asked.

"Not necessarily, Tim. A man's physical characteristics make him unique. The Courtier will, however, utilize his own to their fullest advantage. Obviously, it is to his advantage to maintain some degree of awareness, if his physical form gets out of shape. Again, his self-examination is complete."

"Can he grow a beard?" Alec asked.

"Not by the Professor's standards," Sam commented. "He would make someone uncomfortable."

"I would have to say you're right on that score, Sam," Tom answered. "A beard is somewhat like that gaudy shirt we were talking about earlier. It is most appropriate in the wilderness on a two or three week camping or fishing trip but it is an eye-catcher at any other time. Again, how does our Courtier wish to be recognized? Every man, at some time in his life, tries to grow a beard. A most enlightening experience. The Courtier will have tried while still in school to show his attained manhood before entering into the world of business, or after retirement, so that he can sit around stroking it while making profound statements on the world's obvious demise."

"That settles the matter of a beard," Jack said. "What about a mustache?"

"No question there at all, Jack," Tom answered. "Completely acceptable. Keep in mind the attention getting quality of it. It should not have such an effect."

"You mean no handlebars, or waxed or pointed ends," Sam offered. "To change the subject briefly, Professor," Alec said, "we were wondering last night if you considered the college campus a business environment. Also, are there Courtiers among the faculty?"

"Those are two loaded questions, Alec. Let me answer the first by saying that the campus is approaching a business environment. The monetary return from joint efforts between the universities of this country and the major manufacturers has become so important to the universities that they have had to change their image. At least at the administration level within any university, there is an acceptance of the need for accepted business methods of carrying out their objective. Should they not conform to the ways of the business community, they place themselves in the dangerous position of not obtaining a piece of that glorious action called grants. They must conform.

"Among the faculty, however, we still have the historical image of the academic. As to whether there is a place for a Courtier here, I will ask you a question, Alec. Have you ever met a dedicated professor, who had spent his life on campus, that in any way resembled what we have laid out for the Courtier to attain?"

"I can't say that I have," Alec answered. "Certainly, the average college professor could not teach this course. I just don't feel he would have any of the awareness you have made such an issue in our discussions. Locked into their word of academia, as they are, the realities of the life in the business world just doesn't get consideration."

"Is this why you were brought in to teach this

course, Professor?" Everett asked.

"Professor," Tim interrupted, "I don't feel we should expect an answer to that question. If we, in any way, profess to be Courtiers, we must admit that a question of that type generates discomfort — a feeling we have given more than due justice to in the last few days. Please, let it pass."

"The subject is closed. Thank you, Tim. We have exceeded our allotted time again. If the weather is good tomorrow, we can meet outside, as we did on Tuesday. If not, we will be back here — same time."

"Will you join us for a little refreshment, Professor?" Sam asked.

"Yes, if you will see to it that I get underway toward home by six-thirty."

"Great," Tim said. "We'll guarantee it."

DAY FOUR

THE IDEAL COURTIER

The hour that Tom had spent with the six students last evening after class had been most informative. He was pleased that the group had accepted the course with genuine enthusiasm. From their questions, made pointed by the relaxed atmosphere of the Pub, he had clearly in hand six Courtiers. None had rebelled at the qualifications they had been discussing. Each felt that the target they had established for themselves before arriving here at the University, although determined without consideration of the Courtier's image, would be genuinely aided by the approach outlined in the discussions. They were most receptive.

The weather had not improved and the classroom would be their meeting place again today. He had hoped that one more session could be held outside. There was a distinct advantage to meeting outside a classroom in this course. The subject matter demanded their questioning and the informality of the lawn and shade was stimulating. He did have to admit that yesterday's session in the classroom was open and constructive.

The six were in place as he entered the classroom. Again he noted, they had not changed their seating arrangement.

"Good afternoon. I assume you all retired to your rooms for study at a reasonable hour last evening."

"Not really Professor," Sam responded. "We ordered sandwiches after you left — which was a mistake. We broke up at eleven."

"I do hope you didn't diminish the preparation of your other courses for today. We don't want the Courtier to receive a bad name so early in the summer."

"We spent the evening weighing the graces of the Courtier against what you have called his mechanical expertise," Everett said. "You have pretty well convinced us that his graces will get him further ahead than what he knows about his specialty."

"A totally wrong conclusion, Everett," Tom said. "Obviously, a point that needs clarification."

"You must remember," Tom continued, "that the Courtier's presence could not be justified, nor even permitted, if he did not function with outstanding result in his field or specialty. Keep in mind also that the objective of the Courtier, the target of all his graces, if you will, is the attainment of the highest level position open to any employee. To have that as a target demands outstanding performance in the mechanical specialty that his present title affords. Under no set of circumstances could the graces of the Courtier replace any degree of expertise needed to perform the task for which his paycheck rewards him. Possibly the greatest asset a Courtier can have is that he is the best among the many seeking the top. Only with this ability will his added graces be permitted to advance his cause."

"But Professor," Jack interrupted, "he can accomplish so much with his graces, as you put it, that his mechanical expertise will take second place."

"Jack," Tom said, "never forget that the only objective of business is the bottom line. In attaining quality in that line, the use and function of the Courtier is most welcome, but under no circumstances can the Courtier's graces be a substitute for an outstanding performance of the mechanical function. In any instance, and you can recall your own personal case, recognition first arises from performance of the mechanical function. At all stages of your advancement you will be expected to be worthy of the use of your graces as Courtier. That worthiness will be evaluated solely on your contribution to that bottom line. That is the only reason for your existence in any company. The quickness by which your tenure can be terminated will surprise you, if you look realistically at the mode of good business practice. With all of the value that we ascribed to the Courtier, we have innately assumed that his qualifications in his mechanical specialty were outstanding. Nothing less can be permitted."

"Then the graces of the Courtier," Alec commented, "will have little benefit to one who is second rate in his mechanical specialty."

"There is always benefit from such graces, Alec," Tom responded. "No matter where in the business world or outside of it you find yourself, the graces of the Courtier will be of true value. They are the graces of a gentleman, and have place in any environment. What we are emphasizing is their value in the business community. We cannot, however, substitute them for mechanical specialties."

"We had our Courtier performing all manner of miracles last night, Professor," Tim said. "We had given him all of the attributes you discussed and realized his strength. His potential for power by his mere strength was awesome. I guess we went overboard."

"The power," Tom said, "or more realistically the influence of the Courtier can be substantial. We will have much more to say about it tomorrow, as we see him advance into the upper levels of management and attain a position where he has the opportunity to advise. It is here that his true influence comes into focus.

"One last comment on your enthusiasm for the strength of the Courtier is in order. Seldom does one individual attain the perfection that you ascribed to your Courtier's image of last evening. There will be levels of accomplishment, even among those who have the target clearly in focus. Perfection is a fine reference point. I must warn you of not becoming disillusioned with a point of progress somewhat less than perfection. If you pursue the objective as outlined — and we have much more to add to what has already been offered — you will certainly gain some degree of awareness and efficiency in the effort. The doing will entrap you. The objective may become your sole effort. This will be a mistake. You must keep in mind my earlier comment of maintaining a high level of proficiency in your mechanical activity. Loss of it will tear down any effort made to improve yourself by the gained skill of the Courtier."

"It is easy to see what you mean by entrapment, Professor," Frank said. The attainment of these skills you speak of appears to be a fun thing . . . much more enticing than study for the so called mechanical specialty. It would not be hard to generate a one-track mind."

"A fine way of describing the error, Frank, and one that can easily be remembered. A one-track mind usually ends up in a head-on collision. Not pleasant to look forward to."

"What are you planning to add to the Courtier's arsenal today, Professor?" Everett asked.

"I told you that tomorrow we would get into the function of the skilled Courtier — the point where he enters into the advisory capacity. Before we get into that discussion there is a facet of this Courtier concept that needs explanation and will certainly command curious inquiry. It resides in the consideration of women as Courtiers, and where and how they can function."

"You're planning to open a real can of worms, aren't you?" Tim asked.

"I don't see it as such, Tim. What I do see, and I am sure each of you has been aware of it for some time — women are in the workplace to stay. They are working diligently to assure themselves of fixed positions and in so doing expect and will acquire positions of authority. Our consideration of their presence will be restricted to the graces they should seek and the Courtier's relationship with them, as professionals. You will be faced with the situation at some point in the near future and you should be familiar with what you must look forward to in the encounter."

"By definition, Professor," Everett said, "I see no way that a woman could be a Courtier."

"By strict definition, Everett, you are right," Tom said. "Yet, there is much within the Courtier's makeup that can apply to women. Our suggestions for manners, speech, and cultural pursuits would certainly be most necessary, should she wish to function in the business community. The grace attained from their mastery would be no less valuable to women than to men."

"The mastery of the graces has no bearing on how a woman can function in the business world," Jack said. "She is in no way equipped to match the ability of the trained Courtier."

"Where in hell is she going to fit into the need concept we spent so much time discussing?" Tim asked.

"I would think," Alec said, "that she would fall more into the want category."

"Obviously, there is no question that she has many hurdles to overcome," Tom said.

"That is not the point, Professor," Sam said. "The point is that she just doesn't fit."

"The point is, Sam," Tom responded, "that she is in the work place and fit or not, she is determined to stay. She has also had a measure of success."

"But she is being used," Alec commented.

"Is not the Courtier used, Alec?" Tom questioned.

"I suppose, so, but in a different way," Alec answered. "He expects to be used. He has trained himself for the prospect and is prepared to adjust to whatever arises. I don't see that is possible for a woman."

"There are many ways to use, Alec," Tom responded. "The woman in business will have capabilities that are not found in the man. They can be used. Capabilities that are not associated with her sexual attractiveness. She, as woman, has quality that is unique. There will be times where these qualifications will be more effective than those of the Courtier. Our world has changed, and business is changing with it. Products and services are being developed and offered in ways unseen in past years. These developments offer women a place in the market and they have grasped at the chance to perform. You will be working with them. You should be able to make distinctions on how to cope with their strengths and weaknesses. You will also need to know what they should possess in the categories that we have discussed here in the last few days — for their own advancement."

"You want us to know how to handle them," Frank said. "Is that it?"

"Partially," Tom answered. "But there is more. We have discussed the qualities of the Courtier and from them deduced what a Courtier is or should be. At this point in time, each of you is striving or will strive to attain those qualifications, assuming you desire the advancement possible within the system. With success, you will move into positions where you will be making judgments about qualifications of others. If they are men, you will certainly be prepared to judge with honesty and a level of experience that makes your judgment worthy. If they are women, you will need a slightly different set of criteria, and it is to this end that we should pursue our discussion here."

"That time frame, Professor, could be extensive," Everett said, "I am more interested in how we handle them on the way up."

"Everett has a point, Professor," Alec said. "In the field of journalism, where I seek my bread, women are evident in large numbers and growing."

"There are more potential bridge builders coming

out of engineering school today that are women than we have seen in the past," Tim said.

"Worrying about them years from today is fine but like Everett said, Professor, the problem is today, not ten years down the road."

"The numbers are not the problem, Tim. If you recall, we spoke at the beginning of this course of the few spots available at the top in any company or organization. The entire purpose of the Courtier's training is to be qualified for evaluation for one of those few spots. Among the women coming into the workplace the yardstick is no different, only the number of potential candidates will be less, in that at this point in time their numbers are less. You are convinced now that the Courtier's position is both unique and most difficult of attaining. It is no less unique nor difficult for the woman who is willing to make the effort to be in the running for the few top positions available. Your competition, if that is what is bothering you, will be small in number but certainly worthy if the individuals concerned approach the task with the same awareness of need that you as Courtiers will. They will be qualified. The differences, and they are solely those evident between ladies and gentlemen, will not necessarily make the success factor significantly greater."

"Basically, what you are driving at, Professor," Sam said, "is that we should be able to identify a woman who has the qualities of a Courtier, to whatever degree that is possible in a woman."

"Exactly, Sam," Tom answered. "And I might add that your comment defines what we have to do in this discussion. Acceptance of their presence and awareness of the reality of their effort and potential for movement up the ladder, may not be to your liking . . . but you had better, as Courtiers, be in a position to cope with their presence and to do so you must be absolutely certain of their identification."

"Will they not stand out as the Courtier does," Jack asked.

"Not really, Jack," Tom answered. "At least not in the early stages. They are, as women, different. You will observe them first as women. You will not necessarily be looking for traits that show strength. Not in the same way you observe men. You can be deceived."

"You will admit that they can perform some of the functions of a Courtier," Alec asked.

"Absolutely," Tom responded. "Conversational ability, cultural awareness, excellent personality — not characteristics reserved for the male. As to the physical activities, they need not take part. They have the feminine character to substitute for these, and in many cases the substitution can be most charming."

"Do the same rules hold for the female?" Everett asked.

"What rules?" Tom questioned.

"Oh, take conversation for instance . . . speaking when not invited, butting in, domineering a conversation . . . things of that nature."

"Those rules are universal, Everett," Tom answered. "But even so, a woman is unlike man and her approach must be different. Above all, she must retain that difference. Should she attempt to mimic man, she will put herself in that position of not having the identity that can be so useful. She must retain her femininity."

"You don't think that women who attempt to dress and act like men can be successful?" Frank asked.

"I am not saying that they cannot be successful,"

Tom answered. "What is evident is that by their attempt to approach man in appearance and mimicked characteristics, they set aside their greatest strength — the softness of woman. This natural characteristic is armor. Take it off and they become vulnerable. The strength of true femininity is renowned."

"It is necessary for the Courtier to understand that woman has few ways to defend herself from the onslaught of man. Within the business community she cannot compete in ways that the Courtier is trained — in combat. She will, if she retains her femininity, have equally effective weaponry and the Courtier must be on guard."

"There is no question that she is going to be left out of much of the activity that normally is associated with the business community," Everett said. "She can't join men on the golf course, the ball field, or the football field. She has to be left out of such activities."

"It is not that she can't, Everett," Tom said. "It is that she should not. There are many women who have proficiency in those and other sporting activities. To enter into direct competition with men makes of her a loser, no matter how she performs — at least within the business community. If she wins or out-shines men on the playing field, she incurs their hostility. If she loses, she is held in contempt for her efforts. If she must compete, she should select other women as companions. Among men, she must keep herself aloof to such temptation and reflect the femininity that is so valuable."

"No matter how you slice it, Professor," Tim said, "she is to be left out of much of the stream of activity that we have spent so much time discussing. She is bound to have a hard time competing."

"From the few high profile business women I have come in contact with," Alec said, "they want the rules changed. Will the rules be changed to accommodate them?"

"I don't profess to know what the future will bring, Alec." Tom answered. "What we see is the acceptance of their presence with sufficient adjustment in demeanor to permit their functionality among men. It is difficult to see where they can be taken in to complete confidence. There is much that men will not nor cannot discuss in the presence of women. This places them at a distinct disadvantage. Where they have been successful, they have done so based on their excellence in some particular field, where the normal methods of progress have been set aside to accommodate them. Even in these cases of successful upward movement, the system has had to change."

"So they do operate with different standards," Frank asked. "They have managed to get the rules changed?"

"In cases where they are present, Professor," Sam asked, "does the Courtier's function change?"

"Not as he is evaluated by his superiors," Tom answered. "The Courtier is still Courtier in that context. His relationship with women will certainly demand adjustment in his approach to them but not to those who need his services."

"You spoke of women attaining success where excellence in a specific mechanical function was sufficient to move them ahead," Everett said. "Having such excellence in a mechanical function and then acquiring the graces of the Courtier in the areas where such acquisition is appropriate — say conversation, culture, all social graces — they will become extremely attractive entities. The Courtier, having similar qualities is most apt to be drawn to such an entity,

Is he not Professor?"

"A most worthy match, Everett," Tom responded. "Also, for both, a most dangerous encounter."

"You mean that love and leadership do not mix," Jack said.

"No, they do not, Jack," Tom answered. "I need not go into details of mixed relationships in business. You are all certainly aware of the problems that come from them, in a general sense. If we keep our discussion solely on the Courtier and his involvement with women of outstanding ability and position within the company, we can constructively add to our Courtier's value and garner a more worthy understanding of women's place in such circumstances."

"We must keep clearly in mind the objectives of both," Tom continued. "They are seeking recognition. They desire to attain higher levels of position and prestige. They demand advancement and are willing to do what is within reason to attain it. It makes little difference that one is above, equal to, or beneath the other in position or title. When they come into contact, emotional involvement is anathema to the furtherance of their objective."

"You certainly make that judgment with assurance, Professor," Tim said. "Why such certainty?"

"The basic nature of the participants, Tim," Tom responded. "Keeping in mind their objectives, the Courtier is not trained in love — the woman is. If the Courtier casts caution to the wind, he will suffer. If the woman does likewise, she will not be able to keep it secret, therefore the relationship must be out in the open — not always an ideal relationship under which to function in a competitive business environment. Both parties become encumbered by the relationship. Neither, then, can function efficiently to continue the pursuit of their target. It becomes obvious that to permit such involvement is not to the benefit of either party."

"That may be easier said than done, Professor," Alec said. "If two people are placed in close relationship on a day-to-day basis, and having the similar personalities that our two contestants do, I don't see any way they could not become involved."

"If their cause is sufficiently strong, they will not let such entrapment inhibit them, Alec," Tom said. "There is a dedication that attaches itself to this Courtier concept and certainly it is evident in any woman who attempts to attain stature in the business environment."

"What approach do you use in such a case, Professor?" Tim asked. "You cannot act out the role of the suitor yet, to get along, if you can use the expression, there must be congeniality. The Courtier is placed by such a set of conditions between the proverbial rock and a hard place."

"The approach you request, Tim, is easily defined," Tom said. "Its implementation and the restraint demanded is far from simple. The approach, and it is equally valid for both parties, is to maintain the arms length configuration in any prolonged encounter. The dedication that each has for his or her objective is strength giving. It must be kept front and center as a guiding light. The quality of value judgment is of profound importance under such circumstances."

"The Courtier, and for that matter a woman of dedication, must be able to set priorities," Frank said. "Is that what you mean?"

"As cold as it may seem, Frank, considering we are discussing the emotions of two human beings, the answer is a definitive yes."

"Are we not in a position here, Professor, of placing inordinate value on success," Everett ask.

"No more so, Everett, than with any of our considerations," Tom answered. "You must have by this time realized that the path of the Courtier is voluntarily chosen. The choice is based solely on the reward seen as a result. It is not our purpose here to make judgments regarding the seen value of that reward. Our task is to assist those who have made the choice. Remember, the perfection acquired by a Courtier is by choice."

"Then it becomes evident, Professor," Sam said, "that there is no need of deceit in relations with women in the circumstances we are considering. The approach is straightforward."

"Exactly, Sam," Tom answered. "The straightforward approach, as you put it, establishes the rule. There is no need for uncertainty and, obviously, no need for deceit."

"You used the expression, ladies and gentlemen, Professor," Jack said. "Those terms just don't seem to fit people in the business community. The concept seems alien to what we all know is a combat zone."

"A good point, Jack — one that deserves comment. The terms, ladies and gentlemen, are simply defined. You seem to be questioning the use of their characteristics in a business environment, knowing that the environment is one of competitive existence. I see no conflict. You must remember that relationships between people need not be vulgarized simply because they are in a competitive engagement. If the competition were physical, the terms would be less easily justified. Whether we consider the competition within a given company or the competition that resides between companies, we are dealing with human relationships. The plan on which these relationships interact in the business community is intellectual. The attainment of the tools necessary to compete are of the intellectual variety. To function in an intellectual environment demands the acquisition of gentlemanly characteristics. Intellectual discourse cannot ensue without such characteristics. If women are involved, ladylike behavior is no less necessary.

"There is so much of our business enacted today in a social atmosphere that the relationships demand the character of ladies and gentlemen in the participants. Without such character, the doing of business would revert to the crudity of physical combat. Not a very pleasant circumstance to envision."

"What is the way of the Courtier, Professor," Everett asked, "when he, as gentleman, is in the position of working for a lady? It would seem that his path would be strewn with rocks."

"Not necessarily, Everett," Tom answered. "Here, attitude is the key. As Courtier, he is fully equipped to make such an adjustment and live within the guidelines established by the system. On the contrary, should he feel such a situation is beyond his ability to function, he is sufficiently the gentleman that he will depart the scene."

"That presents one hell of a choice, Professor," Tim said. "Give up what might be years of effort because a woman takes over as Boss — not a very pleasant alternative."

"Would the choice be any less difficult, Tim, if there were a serious personality conflict with any new Boss, if that Boss were a man? I don't see any difference in the two possibilities. Think back to what we said earlier. The position of the Courtier is one that is chosen. Choice is in the hands of the Courtier under this situation. In either case, he must decide what is best for his own future. Should the potential conflict be beyond his ability to cope, he should depart."

"Where does our consideration of need reside, Professor," Alec asked, "as it applies to a woman as Boss? Certainly, a woman would not call on men to do the things that a man would request from his male employees. If she did, I would suspect things might get rather sticky."

"Surprisingly, Alec," Tom answered, "the requests would be a little different. I am assuming that the woman in question is the lady we are describing. If so, her requests will be just, within the framework of normal business practice, and completely acceptable. I would think that to prejudge the potential in such cases is out of order. Suffice it to say that our Courtier will have the proficiency of trade to handle such an eventuality."

"It would appear, Professor," Everett said, "that you do not see major problems developing from a woman entering upper levels of our business community."

"You are, with that statement, Everett, putting words in my mouth. What I have attempted to convey is that our Courtier is properly equipped to cope with the possibility. He is a gentleman and, as such, will adjust to whatever circumstance he is faced with. His lessor equipped co-workers may not be so fortunate. In their case, the entry of women into the business environment can and in many cases does result in extreme conflict and emotional upheaval. We need not enter into discussion on that subject in this course."

"We have not given any consideration to the appearance of women, Professor," Frank commented. "It would seem that woman's normal concern for proper clothing and other accoutrements, that in the battle zones of business, she would be adequately prepared."

"That will be the case, Frank, if she has taken the time to understand the same set of parameters that our Courtier has — thus, giving her the awareness of the needs of proper clothing and appearance. It is a good point and one we should not neglect."

"Going back to our earlier commentary on women," Tom continued, "we placed great emphasis on her retaining her femininity — primarily to give her the strength to cope in a man's world — since within the realm of femininity lies much strength. Should she try to mimic men in her dress code, she will defeat the value of femininity as she would by mimicking men's habits or their performance in other physical activities. She is not placed in any adverse position by the needs of the workplace for proper attire. The fashion world today is well aware of her needs and offers a wide choice of stylish attire — the propitious use of which can add greatly to her natural endowments."

"That was cutely said, Professor," Sam said. "We might, from your generous complimentary presentation of women in the work place, envision them to be a most delightful addition. I'm not sure that I have reached that most generous opinion as yet."

"I would expect any of you to have reservations," Tom said. "My earnest hope is that you will develop the skills of the Courtier so that if the circumstance arises where you are called upon to relate to women in any capacity, you will be up to the challenge."

"From what has been said so far about women, Professor," Alec said, "given all of the skills we have said she must attain to secure her position, is it not reasonable that she should be called a Courtier?"

"No reason why she shouldn't be, Alec," Tom answered. Custom has tied the word to a concept that fits the male but the true meaning fits women as well. One note of caution — you may not find acceptance of the term 'Courtier,' by women, a safely pronounced assumption. I personally am not convinced they are ready for the assignment."

"I think we have given our Courtier sufficient background on the women in his career who will influence his behavior while in the workplace. Tomorrow, as I told you earlier, we will enter the true workplace of the Courtier — his position of adviser. His potential in that capacity should lend assurance to your understanding. We'll shorten this class today, with the assurance that tomorrow's effort will be extensive and possibly require more than our allotted schedule of time."

"Professor," Sam interrupted, "before we wrap up this session, one more question on women. Do you feel that a woman should be Boss?"

"If the woman is qualified and has the proven ability, I see no reason why she should not attain the highest levels offered to any other employee in the workplace. Queens have ruled with exemplary performance. Women have made wonderful contributions to society over all generations. Their potential in the business community is equal to any that is offered to man. They only have to perform. The criteria for women is identical to that ascribed to men. Such is the present condition of our business system."

"You didn't answer my question," Sam said.

"Let us say that it is wise not to be excessively influential on young minds, who in the long run will have to make the decision themselves."

"Touché!" Sam responded.

"As for tomorrow," Tom continued, "let us hope the weather cooperates. I would like us to meet outside for the last session. We will start our class at 3:30, a half hour later than today, as I welcome our next class at 3:00."

"Will you join us again tonight for a bit of refreshment, Professor?" Tim asked.

"Not tonight, Tim, I had planned to surprise my wife and get home early. Remember my comment of this morning. Do not let the Courtier keep you from your other commitments. We must protect his good name."

Tom got up from his desk and walked to the door of the classroom and departed. The six remained seated and from what he heard as he walked down the hall, there was still no real assurance of the way to handle women in the workplace. They would certainly get little else accomplished this evening.

DAY FIVE

THE IDEAL COURTIER

The second class of six, scheduled to start the course next Monday, had just left the classroom with their Blue Folders in hand. Tom had remained behind, awaiting his present six for the last day of their course.

The weather was hot, humid, and threatening showers. He was disappointed that he could not convene this last class outside. This first group of the season had been most enthusiastic and he felt they were worthy participants for the contest of life in the business community.

This last day of class offering would sum up for them the sought after qualifications of the Courtier and enlighten them on the potential worth of the acquisition. He disliked the idea of starting this most important day at three-thirty in the afternoon, on Friday. If there were any plans in the offing for the students, their anxiety over delay could be disturbing.

They arrived together at three twenty-five, evidently sincere in their professed enthusiasm.

"Sorry for the need of a classroom again today, Gentlemen," Tom said, as they again took their same self-assigned seats.

"No strain, Professor," Tim said.

"Did you pass out those lovely Blue Folders to the new crew?" Jack asked.

"Yes, and they showed no more enthusiasm than you did when I gave them out last week."

"That first day was somewhat of a disappointment, Professor," Sam said. "No one knew what to look forward to. Then, when we read the Blue Folder right after leaving the classroom, we were upset and not certain of our decision to take part in the course. Fortunately, we did and I personally am well satisfied. You have generated more questions than I could have dreamed were possible about the future and our part in it."

"This consideration of women we went through yesterday," Alec said, "made for a wild evening, after yesterday's class. A shame, really, that you didn't join us last night."

"Did the wildness arise from your not having accepted them," Tom asked, "or was there some other reason?"

"Let me say that we have accepted the fact that they are in the workplace," Everett responded for the group. "There is still a great deal we don't know about how to cope with their presence."

"I don't feel that response to that condition is something you can or will receive from instruction," Tom said. "Self improvement in your individual capabilities will enhance your ability to design a solution. Each of you will establish different methods of coping, as you put it, Everett, and extensive discourse here will be of little value."

"There is one area that we would like to pursue briefly, Professor," Jack said. "With women in the upper levels of business management, is there not apt to be a softening of personality among the male members of such a system? And assuming that there is, will the resultant effect be detrimental to a particular organization as it deals with others who are not so structured?"

"Jack, that is a most profound observation," Tom said. "I can see I did miss a good session last evening."

"To answer your question," Tom continued, "and I am not confident that I can — with any degree of precision — it might be wise to consider historical precedent. Where queens have ruled and the countries under their dominance were strong and expansive, there was little question as to the ability of its male leaders, under such a ruler. In the outstanding cases of history, England being a fine example, the queen was a hard and determined ruler. What we do not know of course is the number of men — potentially powerful leaders — who stepped aside because of that female presence.

"The same question would arise in business. Women have led many companies to success. What changes in staff formation were necessary under their dominance is hard to say. You used the word softening, Jack, and I wonder if it is the right description for the situation you propose. The female of the species is and can be quite hard, if you will, when such hardness is demanded to protect her own family. Placing her at the helm of a business organization, considering her need to protect it, I suspect she would do a fine job.

"The fact that she may drive away men who are reluctant to submit to female dominance may not have a net loss effect on the company. Your proposal certainly leaves much to be desired in response but I don't feel qualified with our present experience to further the analysis. We need years of results to call upon. The influx of women into management, in numbers of significance, is too recent.

"You made a hell of a lot more sense out of the question than we did last night, Professor," Frank said. "Suppose we just let you off the hook."

"I have no remorse from that response, Frank. We should get on with our Courtier's escapades. We have much ground to cover."

"When does this advising capability you spoke of begin?" Alec asked. "Can the Courtier, at an early age, have influence?"

"Those two questions, Alec, are in content, the summary of our remaining discussion," Tom answered. "First, you must understand that worth of the Courtier relates not to years but to knowledge and understanding. Occasionally, you will see a very young man move into a high level position — one where the staff around him is much his senior. Why? Solely because he has proved his capability and done so at an early age. Obviously, he made a commitment early on in his career and sought out what he felt were the tools that would give him an edge. His choices were correct. The Courtier must do likewise. His youth, if he has it, will in no way inhibit his growth. Knowledgeable men will seek out knowledge, and the potential guidance forthcoming from it. If the Courtier available is equipped, he will be used. It is that simple."

"In the case of ourselves, Professor," Frank said,

"you have told us we are Courtiers. By your definition, we are on the way, as it were. To what end can we be used in an advisory capacity?"

"Companies and their leaders tend to get locked into themselves, Frank. They need the proverbial breath of fresh air and they need it regularly. A good manager or leader will understand the need and make provision for it. Industry is innovative but it must be fed from outside sources. You have been sent out to increase your knowledge but you will also bring back new ideas. As they are passed on they will be the seedstock for new directions. There may not be a formal exposition of what you have been exposed to here, but with time and opportunity to talk under varied circumstances, your gained knowledge will offer bits and pieces to a new pattern."

"That is mechanical knowledge, Professor," Everett said. "You have made the point a number of times that it is separate from the knowledge of the Courtier. Now you say that it is the source of the advisory capability. I don't understand."

"The strong case we made for the separation of the mechanical expertise of the Courtier from his development of the skills of the Courtier that were non-mechanical had the purpose of showing the difference between the two. If you will recall our first session — we had difficulty separating them. Once the separation was established, the development of the Courtier's non-mechanical skills became understandable.

"The Courtier functions in an environment where his mechanical expertise pays the bills or, more honestly, adds to profitability. It is still the first cause. It cannot be forgotten in any consideration of the business system. We spoke as well of the fact that the ideal Courtier would also, in most cases, be outstanding in his mechanical expertise. Strictly speaking, within a given business environment, there is no separation of the two concepts. You might consider them as partners.

"However, to have the maximum effectiveness, the mechanical skills must be presented with the manner of the Courtier. This image we have given high priority to in our discussions. The system we continually refer to is composed of human elements, not mechanical robots. For any degree of success to flow from this system, communication is the key. The coupling of this concept, communication, with the expertise demanded in the mechanical function, is what separates the Courtier from his kind, making of him a more worthy entity . . . needed and to be used for the furtherance of the unit within the system that reveres his presence."

"Can we measure our progress by the degree to which we are used?" Everett asked.

"Crudely, yes, Everett," Tom answered. "The degree to which one is used, thus needed, can be a measure of progress. The time when the Courtier attains what we call a successful position cannot be measured in days, weeks, months, or years — nor within a place — but at the point where a total presence is established. To attain this presence, where functionality is complete at any stage of his development, we see the realization of the insistence on the acquired broad-based knowledge we have so stressed."

"So there is success for the Courtier, even in his early stages of development?" Tim asked.

"Yes, Tim, and it is this continual reward, offered at every stage of his progress, that gives him the continued incentive necessary to further his cause.

He is never uncertain of his effectiveness . . . and from the awareness he develops the confidence that gives his presence a dominance, easily identified."

"Confidence comes from knowledge," Sam said. "Is this the key you peak of, Professor?"

"Yes, fear of anything usually stems from a lack of knowledge of the subject. With knowledge in place, fear departs, permitting openness of attitude. Frankness is the most wonderful of attributes. It cannot be acquired without confidence and a knowledge that is complete. It permits the bold approach which is so impressive. To attain confidence, boldness of offering, and frankness of presentation, there is demanded of the personality that quiet confidence of mind that comes from adequate feeding. The feeding is the learning process that we have spoken of. It is continual, and each added morsel becomes a virtue that quietly gives self-assurance."

"This quiet self-assurance is the sign that says the Courtier is available for use. It that it, Professor?" Alec asked.

"Precisely, and a most valuable sign it is. It should be worn with pride."

"This boldness and frankness you speak of, Professor," Jack asked, "cannot those attributes be dangerous?"

"Only if practiced with an overbearing presence. If you come on too heavy, to use the contemporary expression, there obviously is danger present. Boldness and frankness that stem from a well of confidence usually comes forth with softness that is completely acceptable — in no way grating. Again, the manner of the Courtier makes acceptable his offering."

"What the Courtier has to say, then, must be constructive," Alec said. "If it is, he is listened to."

"Right, and it is for this reason that he must use extreme caution. As he is questioned and listened to, he must avoid the deceitful, never rebuke nor offer ill words, and consider justice in all offering. It is a simple fact that the workers in many cases are more wise than the rulers. When the worker is given the opportunity to expound, he must do so with gentility. He must please. To gain or retain good will, the Courtier will learn to offer truth with gentle words. His frankness or boldness can be accepted, as they come forth in gentle confidence."

"The guy has to be an actor," Tim said.

"Not really, the Courtier cannot act out his part. Acting is false presentation. Falsehood cannot be part of the courtier's makeup. He survives with honesty. He builds on it. Reality is his only guide. Should he act out any part, he will be trapped in the falsehood that will be made evident. Falsehood cannot be masked. Not for any extended period of time, as its weakness ultimately designs its inevitable collapse."

"I'd like to get all these attributes we are discussing tied to specific cases, Professor," Sam said. "It seems that we are making a lot of generalized statements."

"Of necessity, Sam, we must first speak in generalities," Tom said. "Remember, the rules of the Courtier are not written. His frame of learning and his frame of operation are ever so wide. We cannot give him a list of specifics. We can give him no rules. The guideline he carries is one of generalities. His uniqueness, and ultimately his success, comes from mastery of the general. He is, beyond his mechanical specialty, a generalist. We can and will put him in many special cases for enlightenment but to show effectiveness in those cases where he is called upon for his value, his general awareness is his most profound asset."

"What you are saying, Professor, is that he must always know where he is at," Frank said. "He is always aware of his surroundings and adjusts his presentation to the needs of those surroundings."

"Exactly, Frank. This adjustment, that Tim wanted to call acting, is what distinguishes the Courtier. He doesn't act. He proceeds with designed caution. A most worthy premise for any adventure."

"We haven't ascribed the word cunning to the Courtier, Professor," Everett said. "It would seem that the word might fit."

"Fit it does, one cunning man will suffice for many ignorant ones and it is for this attribute that the Courtier is called."

"Is this cunning a virtue, Professor?" Alec asked. "It has a nasty connotation in my mind."

"Virtues and vices are not ours to evaluate, certainly, not on the moral plane. Cunning is a virtue for the Courtier in the sense of an asset. Place him in a situation where he must advise or respond. Make that situation such that the advisement or the response demanded will be a bitter pill to swallow for whoever or whatever is the subject. Is it not propitious in such a case to find a way to sweeten the pill before administering it? The Courtier will have such awareness and will make the response or offer the advice in such a way that the acceptance of the result will not be painful. He will not inflict pain on any who may be affected by his advice or response. His cunning in handling such a situation is by no means the nasty approach you spoke of, Alec. Our Courtier, by his cunning, has lent comfort, where a less well thought out offering could have inflicted pain."

"He is a diplomat," Frank said.

"You might call him such," Tom said. "In the case of his being cunning, we should make one point clear. His use of the virtue, to consider it as such, is for good, not evil. Through cunning the Courtier will find ways of being constructive, not destructive. This, Alec, may let you consider it as a moral virtue, although from our sense — in defining the Courtier — we dare not enter that realm."

"I can understand your reluctance to discuss the morality issue, Professor," Alec said, "but I wonder if we might not at least consider the appropriateness of moral virtue in the Courtier. With the strength of his potential influence, as he attains positions where such influence can have effective bearing upon those over whom the organization rules, must not his character be of considerable motive force — for good, if it is virtuous; for evil, if it is not?"

"Most certainly it can. We must, however, leave that result to the goodness that arises in man from his acquisition of knowledge. Learning, Alec, is the criterion. The broad based learning that we have emphasized will teach our Courtier what is demanded of man in the making of decisions based on justice. His approach will be tempered by his mastery of the arts, and the learning he has given such effort to attain. Evil filters out of ignorance and with the development we ascribe to our Courtier's cause, ignorance will not be his companion. We are attempting to give our Courtier effectiveness through the acquisition of knowledge. His development will lead him toward good from such knowledge. The degree of that good or the danger of evil will follow from the completeness with which he pursues the cause which he has set out for himself."

"You don't fear evil in the Courtier, if he honestly

seeks the title," Jack asked, "and ultimately earns it?"

"Not in the least, the completeness in the man, when he attains the result he seeks, will make justice his companion."

"Speaking of companion, Professor," Frank said, "our Courtier must be a companion to his Boss if he is to advise. When does he move from the position of occasional sounding board to this position of companion?"

"To give you a short answer, Frank — when he earns it. There is no way to put time frames on such happenings. The result of the Courtier's effectiveness is as much measured by the personality of the Boss, as it is by the correctness and value of the Courtier's offering.

"The degree or extent of usage of the Courtier by his superior can vary widely. Many leaders want extensive consideration and input on any subject before decision-making is demanded. Others ask for and accept very little input, relying on their own innate keenness to guide them. With the open minded superior, the Courtier can have much input of varied nature and add measurably to a superior's thinking. To the other, the one who seldom asks for input, when such is requested the response becomes singularly significant. Here, a brief statement or commentary may be the only requested or permitted offering.

"Again, the Courtier's ability to offer precise commentary becomes most effective with the superior who relishes the minimum in suggestion or advice. The accessible leader — the one to whom our Courtier may become a companion — gives ample opportunity to developed input. To move from the occasional sounding board, as you put it, Frank, to that of companion, is a logical progression, accepting if you will, the quality of the Courtier's skills. He fits. He can be an asset, socially. He is a most welcome addition to any gathering and as such becomes a regular member of the superior's circle of associates. His constructive offerings become more sought after and he moves into the circle of the source of internal knowledge of the organization. Whether he becomes a companion or not depends on the personality of his superior and possibly the age difference between them. The Courtier can be an advisor without becoming a companion. The age difference between the superior and our Courtier may be such that companionship may be difficult. This does not mean that our Courtier is ineffective. He can, with intelligent presentation, accept the breach in age and offer worthy input that a much older person can accept with dignity."

"These words we are using, Professor," Tim said, "advice, input, commentary, all seem to have a nebulous meaning. Can we be more specific?"

"Tim has a good point, Professor," Sam said. "I'm having trouble thinking of things that the Courtier may offer outside of his mechanical specialty."

"Obviously, in his early development and in his first contacts with any superior his input and advice or commentary will be limited to the arena in which his mechanical specialty applies," Tom responded. "As his value is seen, he will be sought for more diverse input. If you consider the function of the leader, you will see clearly where the need of the Courtier becomes part of an organization. Aside from the mechanical function of any company, there is the organization of the people who compose it. Realistically, this part of the leader's responsibility is of greater demand than the mechanical operation. In the management of people, any leader appreciates and many demand large doses of advice, commentary, and suggestion, before settling on a direction. To this end, the leader seeks out the Courtier — the one who will constructively add to his gathering of information and ideas, thus making his decision-making process more constructive.

"In such case, the Courtier can have a most profound bearing on how a leader functions. He can improve the leader's role as manager. He can improve the manager's role as leader. By simple suggestion, he can bring his superior to think in terms of how a given decision will affect the herd over which he acts as shepherd. The press of business clouds the mind of a ruler and he needs to be advised of his possible omissions. Gently done, by the Courtier with grace, such advice can deter great trauma. At the least it can avoid the possibility of individual hurt or destruction of a given employee or inhibit the generation of an attitude of perceived unkindness. These cases of need from a trusted Courtier come to light only if the Courtier is awake and aware. His objectivity, not having to make the decision himself, gives him the presence of mind to look at effects forthcoming from any decision that may not have immediacy to the one making the decision. To an honest leader, this ability of a Courtier is what brings him to a position of prominence. His value becomes immeasurable. His position becomes more worthy with each offering of substance. His reward from the experience prepares him for the time where he will give up his own title of Courtier and take on the one of leader."

"Does the Courtier always have to think in terms of one day becoming Boss, Professor?" Everett asked.

"Is that not your objective, Everett? Is it not the objective all of you seek? We have been speaking of the Courtier as a person, one to whom we have ascribed many attributes and hoped for skills. Have you not yet seen this person as yourself?"

"He is becoming such a role model, Professor," Alec said, "that I wonder if we aren't beginning to fear him? At times, I think of him as an awesome presence."

"He certainly could be an awesome presence, Professor," Jack said. "This is what we made of him last night. Giving him all of the attributes we could recall discussing up until yesterday was bad enough. Now that we have given him this advice and suggestion power, he does become a fearful entity."

"He need not be feared," Tom said. "Respected, honored, and being the role model you spoke of Alec, should not make him feared. He is one to be admired. To get back to your question, Everett, he does continually think of one day being Boss. He must, or how will he select for himself the avenues of learning necessary to do the job? He must put priorities on his effort, as we spoke of earlier. To do so, he must study his superiors and observe what it is that they possess that has brought them to power.

"The good Boss, if we can use the expression, will be a strong leader. He will, by being great himself, make greatness a part of others. He will teach by example and the Courtier will by his training in awareness miss not the opportunity to garner from this man the value offered by the association. Certainly, he will separate the good from the not so good and keep unto himself that which is worthy for his own use in the future. From a leader who commands with impressive leadership, he will acquire the ability to command himself. He learns quickly, that he who can command is always obeyed. Is he not then, Everett, constantly thinking in terms of the day he rules?"

"His cause, that we spoke of yesterday," Frank said, "lies truly in the desire to attain the top. He really has no desire to be a Courtier. Is that it, Professor?"

"You are bordering on the chicken and the egg concept, Frank," Tom answered. "Bosses come about in many ways. Some make themselves Boss by starting a business. Some are bred into the title by being the offspring of owners. A few attain the title through the bedroom. Most, however, climb the ladder. It is here, where the ladder is being climbed, that our Courtier's skills are so necessary. He may at first have no awareness of what the title or job of the Boss entails. He steps into the contest or on the first rung of the ladder and with the awareness we have spoken so much about, begins his work. He establishes his cause and deviates from it only when such deviation has advantage — such as a move to another ladder. Has not your own performance reflected that approach?"

"It is going to take some time to assimilate what we have been discussing, Professor," Everett said. "I keep trying to ascribe these qualities and aspirations to myself, but I find so many obstacles in my thinking that they have not yet found a home."

"I can't picture myself sitting alongside of a swimming pool or walking on a golf course with the President and having him ask for my advice," Tim said. "I need one hell of a dose of ego to make that image have any semblance of reality."

"The simple admission of the possibility is your

answer, Tim," Tom said. "It is not ego that will make it happen, nor is it ego that will make the consideration worthy of the effort. It is work. Work for a cause.

"The Courtier is willing to extend himself beyond all others in the effort necessary to prepare himself. He sees, as others do not, the needs demanded of the Courtier and works diligently to attain them. He knows, almost instinctively from his observations, that if he puts in place the needs he sees, he will be called on for his value. He wants to be needed, as he wants to be Boss. Unlike the chicken and the egg analogy, he knows which comes first."

"Where, or how, or when, do these bits of advice first become needed or their request first seen by the Courtier, Professor," Jack asked.

"What you are really asking, Jack, is when does the Courtier first begin to function? I think that each of you could answer that by looking back on our own brief history in the workplace. When were you first taken out of the shell of your mechanical specialty and exposed to something other than that specialty? When was conversation with you first offered on a subject other than your specialty? When did someone in authority attempt a determination of your non-specialty abilities?"

"You mean when we were first thought of as something to be used?" Sam said.

"Put it another way, Sam. When were you first looked upon as something that might be useful. First, place the horse before the cart."

"Like someone said yesterday, Professor — and it might have been me — that is a damned cold way of looking at things," Alec said.

"Alec, the business community is cold," Tom responded. "Cold in the sense of ultimate reality. Certainly, no organization designed to produce a profit can function as a charitable institution. Each component within its makeup must have a profit content. It must be usable for the end result of the planned venture. Why do you think you were hired?"

"That coldness that Alec speaks of, Professor," Jack said, "resides only at the top. Is that your message?"

"It is not a message, Jack. It is something you must accept. I am certain you have been aware of it right along. The reality is universal. In a communal atmosphere, and really, that is what exists in a business environment, the participants seldom think in terms of profit. They think only of their own surroundings and the conditions they face daily. They look at their effort and feel they should be better paid. They see the management team as a distant entity who has more of life's gifts than they. Consequently, they feel they are not being adequately rewarded. The management team becomes an adversary.

"Two separate worlds exist in the company. If a member of the work force is taken into the management team, he is lost to the community and reclassed as adversary. Within the management team we see the true competition develop. Once the members see the potential return from satisfactory profit, they no longer have the communal consideration. They become individuals and not only want a greater share of the profit but are willing to do what is necessary to improve that profit. They have stepped out of the world of goodness, right, and dependence . . . and entered the world of reality. Their mechanical function is no longer sufficient. They need additional tools to continue their upward movement. If they acquire these additional tools, they become Courtiers. If they do not, they remain Flunkies."

"We are back to where we were on day one, Professor," Everett said.

"We are back to where you six are. We have come back to the present, having to do so since we took the Courtier into the realm of the future, as full advisor to his Boss. Jack's question of when does the Courtier begin to function was a good one. When did you begin to function? Answer that question for yourself. You did begin, and your functionality in the capacity of Courtier was to someone worthy. That is why you are here. You are on the way. Have you yet made the full commitment?"

"Without knowing it, I suspect we have," Tim said. "I said a minute ago that I couldn't picture myself advising the President, yet I begin to think that it may just be possible. If he needs the help and I am prepared to offer it, why not share in the reward? Is it that simple?

"It is that simple," Tom answered. "Only, however, if you are prepared."

"If the Boss or President is in continual need of assistance," Sam said, "then he is little different from other employees. He is not the Godlike figure that most make him out to be."

"He is no less human than any other employee, Sam. His distinction lies in what he has in his hands. He holds the reins. He is the driver. And above all things, remember, there can be only one."

"If he is so human," Everett asked, "what makes him so different?"

"Simply, that when he picked up the reins," Tom answered, "he made the commitment to drive."

"But he needs help," Frank said.

"Certainly, he needs help," Tom responded. "And

it is for this reason and for this reason alone, that the Courtier exists."

"This is truly where that need comes from that we were speaking of the other day," Sam said. "If the Boss is human, he is fallible. He needs advice and suggestions on every important subject before he makes a decision. This makes the Courtier's position one of real value, Professor. It also shows clearly the thought in the Courtier's mind of being Boss himself. He knows, as possibly many do not, that the Boss is only human and can be replaced. The coldness that Alec spoke of is not coldness at all, but just plain reality."

"Well put, Sam," Tom said. "Are you all convinced that you are in a position to advise?"

"I don't think there is any question, Professor," Alec said. "We are not yet in the position to advise on major issues of corporate policy but certainly we have the knowledge to offer some input, as you said earlier. Where does it begin?"

"In little things, Alec," Tom answered. "Suggestions for fine tuning. A company is like a sailboat under full complement of sail. It is always in need of trimming. The good Courtier sees the need and either steps in and makes the correction or points out the point of adjustment that can improve the forward motion. The good captain will accept the offering. With each suggested improvement, he sees the forward motion increase and is grateful to the Courtier. With time, there is built up a dependence on the Courtier. Once that attitude is established, the Courtier's worth becomes significant. He also is given more frequent opportunity to advise . . . and his input shows in forward motion of the organization. He is a force for good within the organization. He has power within that organization and one day may have the reins himself."

"The progress is simply stated, Professor," Everett said. "Is it so easily accomplished?"

"Nothing is easily accomplished. The workload demanded to attain such a progression is heavy. It is continuous and it is at times depressing, because of the rate at which it progresses. Discouragement is the Courtier's greatest enemy. We spoke earlier of his need for patience. He must not become discouraged but must continually seek ways to improve his worth. There is no question that in time his effort will be rewarded."

"I like this trimming of the sail bit, Professor," Tim said. How about a few examples?"

"They arise from that well worn word awareness. The Courtier sees a controversy developing — he offers a corrective measure. He sees a staff member in need of recognition — he suggests the doing and offers a means. He sees the destructive effect of the Boss' negligence in some area — he suggests a new direction. He finds the Boss in a receptive mood — he brings up a nagging problem for solution. He finds the Boss in a depressed mood — he offers the new proposal that a staff member has developed. He stimulates where depression has slowed activity. He tempers wherever enthusiasm may cause laxity or complacency. He knows that when there are serious problems within the organization that a full staff effort is demanded, and he pulls them together to attain the most effective result."

"The guy has to be a genius," Jack said.

"To be as effective as you would have him, Professor," Alec said, "I would think he would have to be Boss."

"He is not quite there, yet, Alec," Tom said, "but he feels the power and from it gains added confidence. He may be but one step away."

"Doesn't the Boss feel threatened by a guy that is so aware and effective, Professor?" Frank asked.

"Not really. If he is honest, his only concern is losing the man. When outstanding capability shows itself, Frank, it is not threatening. It is a great asset and is to be used and rewarded. If the company is large enough, the man can be moved and given adequate opportunity to grow. Should the company be of insufficient size to let a man move out into new fields of endeavor, he is usually rewarded in other ways. Occasionally, the potential for reward will not satisfy the need and the man moves on to other more opportune locations. Good men will not let themselves get trapped. Good leaders, will not, on the other hand, stand in the way of any man's advancement. He will feel no remorse when a man reaches his limit within an organization and knows it. He will accept the fact and let him depart, adding blessing and good will to the new opportunity."

"Isn't that cutting his own throat, Professor?" Everett asked.

"It may appear that way, Everett, but the good leader knows the dynamics of the business world and also knows he cannot slow it down. He does not try to fight the system."

"The good Courtier will use the system. Is that the message, Professor?" Jack asked.

"Part of it. When the Courtier reaches the level of which we are now speaking, he is one step away from assuming the title of Boss. He knows it and his Boss knows it. In most cases, the Boss was in the same position himself at one time. He understands."

"What happens to the Courtier when he does take that step, Professor?" Sam asked.

"When the position of Boss is attained, Sam, the Courtier dies."

"You mean that when he is no longer needed, he is no longer a Courtier?" Alec asked.

"By definition of title, Alec, that is true. In the world of business, however, there is seldom a nice clean line of distinction. Few cases exist where the title of Boss reflects complete autonomy. The Courtier function will continue in most cases, even when the top is attained. The title is gone but the memory and attributes linger on. A life so deeply committed and structured to service cannot be wiped out with one step up the ladder."

"Beyond the acquisition of knowledge in a wide field of cultural pursuits, and the familiarity with all of the activities we have spoken of, Professor," Frank said, "it is evident that the Courtier must become familiar with each of the operations, departments, divisions, staff, and people functions throughout the organization. That is one hell of a challenge."

"The Boss did it," Tom said.

"This ladder we keep referring to, Professor," Everett said, "I can see it is of the fire engine extension type — not the little step version we had at home."

"Everett, you cannot let the size of the challenge deter your course. The cause you accept is worthy. The reward will more than justify any effort expended."

"I get the impression, Professor." Tim said, "that you are aiming at our having a professional approach to the job we are doing. By that I mean, we should look more at the whole organization that at the unit wherein we earn our bread."

"You have little choice but to become professional, Tim, unless you are satisfied with being good at what you do as specialist and need no further challenge. You and Everett are engineers. Is that enough, or would you rather be called president of an engineering company? Sam is a chemist. Will he be satisfied with attaining the title chief chemist or would he rather be owner of a chemical company? Frank and Sam, you are business majors. Will you be satisfied at arriving some day at the position of marketing manager or advertising manager or would you rather see the title president on your calling card? As to you, Alec, will copy editor do, or would you rather be known as publisher?

"The Courtier has little choice but becoming professional. He seeks the greatest reward and the highest position available. He strives from the very beginning to do his superior's job better than the superior is doing it. With each step forward he has a new superior. In time, he is seeking to do the top man's job better than the top man is doing it. For this kind of an approach to success, little less than a professional approach is acceptable."

"When can he cease calling himself an engineer, a chemist, a journalist, or whatever, and think of himself as a businessman?" Alec asked.

"Only when he realizes that these individual titles and the work that they demand are only tools," Tom answered. "When did you last hear your President referred to as Engineer, Chemist, Journalist, or Marketing or Advertising man? He is a little God, a little King, President, Owner, or just plain Boss. He needs not the title, Engineer, Chemist, Journalist, Marketing or Advertising man. He is a Professional

Businessman."

"And yet, early on, Professor," Everett said, "you want us to advise him? That is a wide breach to comprehend from where we sit at this point in time."

"Only, if in awe, you consider him as President, Boss, or Owner, King, or Ruler. When you accept him as human, advising him is a most natural function. Your skills and your professional attitude will make the changing of his will or direction to a more suitable configuration — one that from your professional stance is correct — will be not only eminently satisfying but constructive. Here lies the power and appropriateness of the Courtier in business. As was said earlier, his numbers are small but his influence is substantial."

"In functioning in that capacity, especially close to or near the top," Jack asked, "would not the Courtier become somewhat arrogant?"

"That would be his undoing, Jack. Pride and its resulting show of self-esteem is the great enemy of the Courtier. The thinking mechanism of 'I did it' must be set aside for a more constructive concept. 'It must be done.' Our Courtier, or for that matter any degree of Courtiership, relies on the worth of the doing, not on the one who attains the end. In reality there is no end. Each effort or offering is part of a constructing process. There is continual building as the Courtier proceeds. He has no end to look forward to on a daily or weekly basis. His end is always something greater than the parts that must be dealt with on a short term basis."

"Has any other name been ascribed to this function Courtier, Professor?" Frank asked. "I'm not sure I like the word, although it certainly fits."

"None that I am aware of, Frank. Why would you

want another?"

"Maybe only to Americanize it," Frank answered.

"He has a point, Professor," Alec said. "Most of us would not want to be called 'Courtier.' The meaning has strange connotations."

"Strange to whom, Alec?" Tom asked. "To you now, after having gained an understanding or strange to others who have no awareness of what the word conveys?"

"I don't have any hesitancy with the word now," Sam said, "but I'm certain others might snicker at the use of it."

"Is there any real need to ever use the word, Professor?" Everett asked. "I see the word and its applied principles as bordering on a secret. I would think that to be a Courtier, one mst never speak of the objective nor have need to use the term."

"That is a fine approach, Everett, and one that reflects the true concept of Courtier. There is great dignity contained in the approach of silence. We have spoken at length of the grace of the Courtier. It might be a wise consideration to gain understanding of the assurance that such grace comes from dignity."

"Can greatness come from service, Professor?" Sam asked. "Or is this a myth that we have had impinged upon us through our study of the past?"

"I don't see it as such, Tom answered. "Greatness comes forth from the individual. The circumstances of placement are only the incidental. If you look to examples for our Courtier, there are many. But as to the greatness that pours forth from the man, as compared to his placement, consider that Aristotle was Courtier to Alexander the Great."

"I never recall his name being listed among the Courtiers of history," Alec said. "He stood on his own as a man of greatness, as you put it, Professor. A most worthy target."

"I just had a strange thought, Professor," Everett said. "How are we going to discuss this course when we get back on the job?"

"My God, Jack, "no one would believe us!"

"We may never discuss it," Tim said. "We may never again use the term Courtier, yet the concept and the course that gave it to us may lead us to the top. A strange result, Professor, for your efforts."

"That attitude, Tim, clearly proclaims you as Courtiers."

"We are out of time," Tom continued. "If you are disposed to stop briefly for a bit of Friday night refreshment, I'll buy."

"Let's go!" The Courtiers proclaimed in unison.

APPENDIX

THE BLUE FOLDER

WHO ARE THEY?

INTRODUCTION

This brief exposure was prepared as an opening statement for the course, THE COURTIERS OF AMERICAN BUSINESS. For the student about to take the course, its content will be maddening. He will obviously feel demeaned. He will see in its content reflections of many of his fellow workers. He may see himself.

In a sense, it is designed to shock — not the experienced Courtier, but he who is taking his first step up the ladder in the business community.

The cases used are factual — real people acting in the most human of ways. Some know they are true Courtiers — others are acting simply as the Flunky for their leader.

The concept Courtier is the substance of the course you are about to undertake. The distinction between

Courtier and Flunky, you are about to understand. Mastery of the former is your objective.

THE COURTIER IN ACTION — FOUR CASES

Allen, Assistant to the President, was at his desk when the President called just before ten o'clock.

"Allen, the Receptionist just called. The visitors from Germany are in the lobby. You know Hans Gerber. Would you go down and greet them and bring them up here?"

"Certainly. Be good to see them."

Allen met the visitors and escorted them to the President's office. After a pleasant round of introductions and a few words of friendliness, he was dismissed.

The morning dragged and he watched as three others from the staff were called into the meeting with the Germans.

At one minute to twelve, he called the President.

"Jim, I am leaving for lunch. Do you need me for anything else?"

"Are you going alone?" The President asked.

"Yes. Just out for a sandwich," Allen responded.

"Why don't you stick around for a few minutes. You can join us for lunch at the club."

"Fine. Give me a call when you are ready," Allen said.

"Will do."

The feeling of again being needed returned, as Allen rocked back in his chair.

* * *

"You know, Bill, our trip is only three weeks away

and you have not settled on who the third couple will be on the boat," Peg commented.

"I'm worried about Avery," the Boss said. "He has not been feeling well of late and I don't think I can depend on him for crew work. John is great but I need at least two pair of hands on that boat. I don't plan to depend on the women."

"Are you thinking of someone from the plant?" Peg asked, as she poured their second cup of breakfast coffee. "If you are, you should let them know soon, so they can make plans."

"Anyone I choose from the plant doesn't need time to plan. They pray for invitations."

"Who do you have in mind?" Peg asked.

"I'd like Tom on board," the Boss answered, "but he doesn't have a wife and I don't think the other wives would appreciate his having some doll aboard to share his bunk."

"What about Sandy and his wife?" Peg asked. "He puts enough time in to justify an invitation. The guy is always working."

"That is the problem," the Boss said. "He feels he cannot leave. We would have three days of his worrying about the maintenance of the plant in his absence. You remember the last time he came along?"

"Well, who else is there?" Peg asked.

"I was thinking of young Sam Johnson. He has only been with us for about six months but he knows boats and should make a good pair of hands on board. You met him at the club a week ago."

"He didn't have a great deal to say," Peg commented. "His wife seemed nice, although she is so young."

"She can balance off you old gals," the Boss said. "It is late. Sit and finish your coffee. I've got to run. I'll talk with young Johnson this morning."

* * *

The President and the Vice President of Sales got out of the cab at the airport. The Vice President paid the fare and then turned to speak to the President.

"Give me your ticket, Jim. I'll check us in. You want an aisle seat?"

"If possible. I'll be in the Coffee Shop. I also want to call the office."

"Order me a coffee," the Vice President said, as he picked up the two suitcases and headed for the airline check-in counter.

"When the flight was called, the Vice President picked up the tab and paid it on the way out of the Coffee Shop.

Aboard the plane, as they were settling into their seats, the Vice President asked if Jim wanted a magazine.

"Yes. See if they have a copy of *Life*. I missed it at home this week."

Before he left to go up the aisle to the magazine rack, the Vice President took the President's raincoat and put it in the rack overhead. When he returned, he stepped over Jim's legs and settled into the middle seat.

Amenities and service were complete, at least until the flight landed. He would at that point get the luggage and meet the President at the cab stand. The President would have visited the men's room and again called the office.

He said a silent prayer that the baggage would be unloaded quickly, so that he would not keep the President waiting.

* * *

"Are you having Paul come with us to Chicago?"

"Can't do without him," Ace responded. He was seated in front of the President's desk and they were making plans for the three day Product Show during the coming week.

"Make sure he knows that we have the bucks to spend and I don't want a couple of horrors in the suite. If that gang from Continental shows up, they want gals that are attractive and amenable."

"I've already talked to him about it," Ace said. "He called Chicago this morning."

"When is he going out?" the President asked.

He'll leave Monday morning. He'll have the rooms all set up and the gals on hand when we arrive, Tuesday afternoon."

"Where does he get the gals?" the President asked.

"I have never asked. He knows his way around and I don't interfere. It makes no difference if it is Chicago or Los Angeles — he has the contacts."

"Do you think two will be enough?" the President asked.

"I told him to plan on three. At least for Tuesday evening. If we are quiet out there, he can always knock one off. Easier than getting an extra at the last minute — he claims."

"That guy sure knows his way around. How long has he been with us?"

"Eight years. He came in the year after you moved into the front office and I took over sales."

"He sure is an asset," the President said.

"It would be nice if he could sell."

* * *

THE COURTIER'S CHALLENGE

The number, effectiveness, usefulness, and success of Courtiers in contemporary business is directly attributable to the Boss. His personality determines if Courtiers are welcome. There are few operations in business that function without them. If not acceptable at the top in a company, due to a Boss who is so non-people oriented that he will neither condone nor avail himself of the service, the Courtier exists at lower levels.

In most cases, the Boss has come up through the ranks and has seen the need of the Courtier and most likely been one himself. We must admit that to be successful in contemporary business, some degree of service is required along the way to those who control the destinies of those in the workplace. The non-conforming, possibly grating individual, who will not bend to the winds of requirement, seldom advances. He is trapped within the pure qualifications he possesses under his job title. He may be valuable to the company in a mechanical sense but unless he can adjust his ways and flow with the system, he will soon become disenchanted.

On the other hand, the flexible individual assumes the role with enviable ease. If his performance is meritorious, without that effusiveness that makes for dislike, either by the recipient of his effort or those monitoring his performance from the sidelines, his reward can be substantial. A satisfactory effort in his titled position, coupled with a true Courtier's performance in day-to-day service to the right superior, can assure steady progress to the pinnacle of any business establishment. This is the reality of our system. To cultivate the air of the Courtier, implementing the demanded functions with grace, requires no technical training or college background. The root of the function lies within the soul of the doer. It must be natural or the result will not stand the test of credibility. A one time effort, done to satisfy an immediate need, is of little value. The service rendered must be continuous and ever available, as circumstances arise calling for its activity. Constant awareness and search for opportunity is the cornerstone of the exemplary Courtier.

The Boss, whether he be President, Manager, or Owner, must know at all times who he can depend upon. To gain the dependence of the Boss is the Courtier's most cherished reward. With this dependence, he has the opening for all manner of service, either requested or fulfilled by an awake attitude, seeking opportunity.

Reaching the point where dependence becomes evident, the service function leads to need for advice and counsel. At this point, discretion is of paramount importance. Once taken in to the thinking process of the Boss, either President, Manager, or Owner, the Courtier begins to feel the power of his position. Maintenance of discretion will lead to advancement. The system demands it. To know is to rule. To know, becomes the Courtier's strength. All effort expended in years of preparation will at this point in time be fruitful.

It is from this point that most leaders took the step to top level management positions. They had proved their understanding of the system. Because of their background, they will demand from their own Courtiers total commitment, if they wish to follow.

THE FUNCTIONING COURTIER
BOSS WATCHING — THREE CASES

Many who practice this pastime are in no sense
of the word, Courtiers. Boss Watching is a function
of all employees. Few there are, among any group
of workers, who do not keep an eye out for the Boss'
presence and the movement he partakes in, as it
brings him into the visual presence of his employees.
All watch the Boss.

To explain this phenomenon is not part of our
effort. Suffice it to say, that such a universal activity
has its root in the normal guilt complex of workers.
To those who do not utilize the activity to pursue a
Courtier's reward, we have no interest. To those who
watch the Boss to provide opportunity for service,
are those with whom we must deal.

* * *

Ben Johnson, President of the company, walked
out of his office and down the hall, headed for the
office of his Chief Chemist. As he passed the entrance
to the laboratory, Fred Hollings stepped into the hall.

"Hey, Mr. Johnson. How are you today?"

"Fine, Fred."

"I understand you bought a horse?" Fred asked.

"Yes, I brought him to the farm over the weekend,"
Ben responded.

"A stallion, I understand," Fred commented.

"Won't be for long — the way he is acting," Ben
said. "Too much animal for me."

"Be a shame to geld such a beautiful animal,"
Fred said. "I hear he is a registered Morgan."

172

"He is a beautiful animal, and yes, he is a Morgan, but I don't plan to get into the breeding business. I want a horse to ride and enjoy. I don't need his fire."

"I have a gelding," Fred said, to keep the conversation going, as Ben had started slowly to move down the hall.

"Have you? What is he?" Ben stopped and showed evident interest.

"A Quarter Horse," Fred answered. "I have had him for three years."

With the comment, he took out his wallet and handed Ben a picture of the animal.

"He is beautiful," Ben said, as he looked at the picture. I didn't know you were into the Western bit. Have you had him in shows?"

"No. I have been to many of them but not as yet entered. That scene gets to be expensive."

So I understand," Ben responded. "You'll have to come out to the farm some weekend to see mine. You would enjoy the place and maybe give me a lesson in Western riding."

"That would be great," Fred said. "I'd enjoy it."

Ben turned and continued down the hall.

Fred went back into the laboratory, thinking to himself, "I sure would love to spend a day on that farm."

* * *

The Plant Manager walked up to the open office door and leaned against the casing, not stepping through into the President's office. He said nothing to announce his presence, but waited until the President looked up from his work.

"Hi, Adam," the President said. "Got a problem?"

"Not today. The plant is running fine."

"What can I do for you?" the President questioned.

"I heard you had the Lancer people coming in this morning. Most likely taking them to lunch. Would you like your car washed? I have a couple of boys looking for work. It can be ready by noon."

"Good idea," the President responded, as he stood up and walked to the closet to get the keys from his topcoat. "While you are at it, have one of the boys check the trunk for me. See if there is still a full box of golf balls in there. The ones with our logo. I want to give these Lancer boys a few."

"Will do," Adam said, stepping into the office now and taking the keys. "I'll have the boys bring the car around to the front entrance when they finish."

"Fine. And many thanks."

Adam left the office and with evident pleasure went into the plant and took one of the maintenance men off a job and had him get to work on the wash job.

He would check the trunk himself.

* * *

The Vice President of Finance walked briskly down the corridor toward the President's office, ostensibly to question his secretary, whose office was directly across the hall. As he neared the door to her office, he glanced to the left and noted that the President was standing in front of his desk.

"Hey, Jim," he said, "I didn't realize you were back. How was the game?"

"Great. I had a good round."

"Did you do well on the fourth?" the Vice President asked.

"One over par."

"Wonderful. You have always had trouble on that hole. Must be in fine shape today. How was your putting?"

"Like a Pro."

"That practice session you had yesterday must have done you some good."

"I need more of those. Is Pat in his office?" the President asked.

"He was there a minute ago. I'll check."

"Tell him to come in," the President said. "Join him, if you're free."

"Be right back," the Vice President said, as he moved out of the doorway and down the hall to get Pat.

Smiling, he thought to himself, "I sure didn't want to miss this meeting. My timing was perfect."

His performance was common. To accidentally accost the Boss and have him fall for the ruse is a most satisfying adventure. Little did the Vice President know that the President and his Secretary had anticipated his presence, having been schooled in his ways by past performance — now habit.

* * *

The first and most basic knowledge of the Boss Watcher is to know whether or not the Boss is in the office or plant. Should he not be on the scene, it is wise to know where he is and to what purpose his absence is directed. This knowledge will offer opportunity at the time of his return to question or comment on his activity during ths absence. Letting him know that there is interest can be most rewarding and lead to conversation that may offer knowledge, unattained, if not aware of the absence.

The showing of interest in the Boss's outside activity, whether it be business or personal, if maintained over extended periods of time, can generate a personal relationship that will foster growth of the Courtier. Each contact and the subsequent questions and answers leads to familiarity, the foundation of a relationship of absolute necessity, if the Courtier is to increase his need to the Boss. This increased need is the nourishment of success.

If the Boss's absence from the office or plant was for business reasons, questioning should be on the result of his effort. If the effort was fruitful, he will be pleased to offer pleasant commentary. If the effort was disappointing, he will be most receptive of a shoulder to cry on. In either case, the level of familiarity will be fostered.

Regarding personal activity away from the office, a knowledge of his activity is helpful. If he was golfing, then an awareness of the proficiency of his game and the course he played is helpful (as used by the Vice President of Finance — Case Three). Such knowledge must be acquired by the Courtier if he is to arouse the interest of the Boss.

In the case of golf, the Courtier must be a golfer. If the Boss had been sailing, and questioning on his return is to be fruitful, the Courtier must have a knowledge of boats. Developing a conversational skill in a wide area of activities that are the interests of the Boss is demanding. These skills are the tools of the Courtier. To many, they are easily attained. To some, there is evident difficulty in gaining a proficiency level that will be of value. Obviously, it is not possible to attain proficiency in all areas that will promote growth for the Courier. He must, however, attempt to become widely educated in the subjects needed for his particular venture. Each Boss has unique likes and dislikes and partakes in different activities. To study his pattern and then develop skills that mesh with his interests, is the curriculum most rewarding.

BOSS HELPING — THREE, CASES

The most common helper is one who handles errands for the Boss — the Errand Boy. The Finder of Needs seems to take the next spot and the one who takes on projects — the Manager of Projects — resides at the top. Each has a value. Each has a level of respect. To each will the Boss be drawn, as proficiency is attained. To work up the ladder from Errand Boy, to Finder of Needs, to the Manager of Projects, is the road to success.

* * *

"Come in, Jim," the President said, as he looked up from the desk. "I need a favor."

Jim was Sales Coordinator and the President had just called him and asked him to come to his office.

"Peg's golf clubs are in the trunk of my car. She has a game this afternoon and I can't leave. I have the Lowenstein people coming in this morning and I'm certain we will go to lunch. Can you break away for an hour and take the clubs out to the house?"

"No problem," Jim answered. "It is quiet this morning and I would enjoy the ride. Is Mrs. Olsen at home?"

"Yes, I just spoke to her. She'll be expecting you — might even make you some lunch."

"If I leave now, I'll be there just about noon."

"When you get to the house," the President said,

"you can do me another favor. Throw my lawn mower in the back of your station wagon and bring it back to the plant. I want the boys in the shop to see if they can make the damned thing start without causing a coronary. It has been giving me fits."

"Is it in the garage?" Jim asked.

"No, I left it alongside of the driveway. You'll see it as you pull in."

"Have you told the boys in the shop what you want done?"

"Haven't had a chance this morning. Been too busy. When you drop it off, you can tell them it needs some kind of an adjustment."

"I'm on my way," Jim said, as he left the office.

"Thanks," the President said, as he looked back to the work on his desk.

*   *   *

Frank walked into his office just before five. He had been out of the plant for two days. His trip had been fruitful and he was anxious to talk to the Boss.

He slipped off his jacket and draped it over the chair. Out of his briefcase he took a small package. He left the office and climbed the stairs to the Executive Level, hoping that he could catch the Boss alone.

He was out of luck. The Boss' door was closed. He stepped into Anne's office, the Boss' secretary, and laid the package on her desk.

"How was the trip?" she asked.

"Great. The Old Man is locked up with somebody, I see."

"Yes. He has been in there for a couple of hours. Some people from the bank. What do we have here?"

178

"Open it," Frank said.

Anne unwrapped the package. It was heavy. It contained two velvet covered boxes, each four inches square. Before raising the cover on the first, she looked up to Frank and smiled.

"You found them?"

"Yes, I found them. In a little shop in Chicago. I hope they are what he wants."

Anne had opened the first box and taken out the ashtray. She set it on the desk and opened the second box. A matched pair of crystal cubes, deeply cut. They reflected the overhead flourescent light and it gave a multicolored appearance to their surface.

"They are beautiful. Just what he has been looking for. He will be real pleased."

"Tell him I'm back, will you. I'll be in my office for a while. I'd like to see him before he leaves."

"Be patient, Frank. I'm sure he'll see you."

* * *

Barry looked up, as the President walked into his office.

"Hi, Marvin. I thought you had visitors?"

"I did," Marvin responded. "They just left. Are you busy?"

"Just logging yesterday's production. What can I do for you?"

"Young Paul came home over the weekend. He shocked both his Mother and myself by driving up in an old beat up 1957 Chevrolet. The damned kid traded his Camero for it.

"I can understand why," Barry said. "Those 1957 Chevrolets are classic."

"They may be, but this thing needs a lot of work.

That is why I am here."

"You need a good mechanic?" Barry asked. "I'd love to work on that car."

"I had something like that in mind," Marvin responded. "I was thinking that if Paul brought the car here to the plant, he could put it in the warehouse next to the shop and work on it inside. If I let him use the garage at home, my own car will be outside all summer. Besides, I'm sure he doesn't have the tools necessary to do what he plans."

"That would be fine," Barry said. "There is plenty of room out there and the boys in the shop would enjoy giving him a hand."

"I want him to do the work himself," Marvin said. "He needs the experience. I don't want him interfering with the shop crew."

"He won't be a problem," Barry said. "Do you know what he plans to do?"

"He is talking about an engine overhaul and a paint job. He may have the damned thing here for weeks. I'm not even sure he can get parts."

"Parts are no problem," Barry said. "I'm sure I can get him what he needs. We can pull the engine right out of it and put it in the shop. Should be fun."

"You sound enthusiastic," Marvin said.

"Hell, I'll get as much kick out of it as he does. Right down my alley."

"I kind of thought it would be," Marvin said. "Give him a call at home, will you, and let him know it's okay to bring it in this afternoon."

*　*　*

Errands run the gamut from getting the Boss a fresh supply of staples for the dispenser on his desk —

normally handled by his secretary — to meeting his Playmate for lunch — advising her that the Boss is unavoidably detained and graciously keeping her in the fold. This errand is given only to the Courtier of utmost integrity.

Between these two extremes range a whole litany of projects for the Errand Boy. Each must be carried out with proficiency. Some require speed. Others demand exactness. In the case of the disappointed Playmate, the most sensitive of personalities is demanded. For each, the Courtier must develop a nonchalance that is appropriate to the task. To be strained in such activity will certainly not permit exemplary performance. The doing requires understanding and a method that lends comfort to the one demanding the service. When this comfort is established, the growth of the Courtier is assured.

The Finder of Needs has a more difficult assignment. He may be asked to perform some simple search, like finding desired accoutrements for the Boss' office or wardrobe or he may be asked to enter into the most personal relationships by assuring companionship for the Boss during his future visit to some city away from homebase. The first case will be rewarded by effusive thanks, done in the presence of others to show gratitude and recognition. The second, may offer sharing or comradery that will be most pleasant and of longstanding value to the Courtier.

As with the Errand Boy's efforts, there lies between these two examples of the Finder of Needs, unlimited numbers of tasks that serve. In all cases, it must be remembered, that to serve is the objective. In many cases, the service is performed to save the Boss time, that is to him most valuable.In others, the Courtier becomes a tool to perform a task not readily accomplished by the Boss. The value placed on each by the individual demanding the service will vary, depending on his personality. It is to the Courtier with awareness that the choice becomes so critical. Having, through awareness and the study of the personality being served, attained a position of confidence sufficient to be asked into the personal life of the Boss, certainly elevates the Courtier to a level of prestige that can be most beneficial in assuring advancement.

To accept assignment to a project for the Boss establishes a long term relationship — a most rewarding opportunity. It can embrace something simple, as gathering together the contents of a tackle-box for a weekend fishing trip or searching out guides and possible lodging for a two-week trip to the north country for salmon fishing. In either case, a number of contacts with the Boss are necessary and much opportunity is granted for improved familiarity. Either case can assure future project assignment, if the service rendered is satisfactory. Certainly, to be asked into the project required previous performance of some task that gave grounds for confidence.

The Courtier attains his stature and expertise not by single acts of service. He must show growth and an ever active willingness to move ahead into areas of more demanding service. Confidence in his ability grows slowly. When attained, his position can only improve. As he becomes more of a crutch to the Boss, he moves into the personal life that is so fruitful in its offering of knowledge. Again, the Courtier must never cease to understand that knowledge is power.

"Take Me Along" is the unspoken dream of the aspiring Courtier. To be with, to travel with, to share with, to play with, to visit with, to eat with, or to in any way be the sidekick of the Boss is the result of proven effort to develop the credentials of the Courtier. His stature rises with each accompaniment. Rises in the sight of his fellow employees and in the potential offered by the activity in his future growth to positions of influence and power. Having attained the right to join the Boss establishes his pre-eminence among his peers.

* * *

Alex Swenson, a young engineer, joined the line in the company cafeteria. He was late. There were only two other employees in front of him. As he stood awaiting his turn to pick up a tray, the President of the company and two guests walked up in back of him. He turned and greeted the President.

"Hello, Mr. Abrams."

"Alex Swenson," the President said. "How are you? Running late for lunch?"

"Yes Sir. We had a trial on the main unit this morning and it took more time than we had planned."

"Did it go well?" The President asked.

"It looks great at this point. We won't have all the data in until late this afternoon."

"Alex, have you met Frank Eden and Jeff Appleby? They are from Keystone Plastics."

"Haven't had the pleasure," Alex said, accepting handshakes from both, with pleasant greetings.

"They are here to see the results of that run you

had this morning," the President said. "It could be of real value to them, if all goes well."

"They can be encouraged," Alex said. "From what we have seen, the results should be favorable."

"Are you alone?" The President asked.

"Yes," Alex answered.

"Why don't you join us. Give us a chance to go over the results of the run and you will get to know these boys."

"Fine," Alex responded.

As he completed filling his try, Alex stepped aside to let the President lead the way into the private room that was set aside for him and his guests.

For Alex, this would be a first.

* * *

The phone rang on Elliot's desk. He was General Manager of the Lake Charles, Louisiana, plant.

"Elliot?" The voice on the line exclaimed, "Jim. How is the goose shooting?"

Jim was President of the company and had his office in Akron, Ohio.

"Great. When are you coming down?"

"How would next Thursday set with you?" The President asked.

"Just fine. Will you be in for the weekend or just a couple of days?"

"I can only afford two days. We'll be leaving for home on Friday night. I thought I'd bring young Frank along. He has been asking for the last two years to ride along. It's time I gave him the opportunity."

"I've never met the boy," Elliot said. "What is his size? I need to get boots and clothes for him. What is he, fourteen now?"

"Yes, he's fourteen and big. Size ten boots and large in the clothes size. Anything will do. Don't make a big deal out of his needs. He is just along for the ride. He won't have a gun."

To himself, Elliot said, "Thank God for that." To the President, "We'll fit him out just fine. Are you coming in Wednesday night?"

"Yes, and plan to have dinner with us. Bring Meg along. She'll enjoy talking to young Frank. Will he need a license to ride along in the boat and be in the blind?"

"No, that won't be necessary," Elliot answered.

"See you Wednesday at the airport. Delta, at seven thirty."

Elliot hung up the phone and sat back in his chair with a sigh.

"To nursemaid a fourteen year old kid in a duck blind," he thought to himself. "For this, I don't get paid!"

* * *

The Boss had just started his car. On his way to work, he had not as yet backed out of the garage. His wife stepped through the door from the kitchen and walked up along side of the car. He lowered the window.

"We have Emery and his wife coming in for dinner tonight. They are bringing their oldest boy with them. Do you want to invite somebody from the plant to join us?"

"A good idea. Tom is in town and his wife is a doll. I'll talk to him this morning."

"What about Dave?" His wife questioned.

185

"Scratch Dave," the Boss answered.

"Really? Is he in trouble?"

"Won't be with us long."

"I will miss having him around. He was such fun. Always made an evening pleasant."

"I'll miss him in the office. He livened up a meeting. He also has turned out to be useless. You know Tom . . . and his wife will fit nicely."

"Oh, Tom is fine. Do you think he will be able to join us on such short notice?"

"You're kidding? He'll jump at the chance."

"You are always so sure of your men."

"I know them. See you tonight."

*　*　*

Joining starts out with brief encounters — for a Coke in the cafeteria, a ride to work in the morning, deliverance at home in the evening, a pickup at the garage where a car is being repaired — encounters that show interest and potential for more in-depth accompaniments. As the relationship between Boss and Courtier becomes more relaxed, service to the Boss becomes more frequent.

An invitation to lunch breaks another barrier on the way to growth. If repeated, and then becomes regular, the Courtier entrenches his position. These are significant steps to fulfillment.

His credentials are being tested. Is he companionable? Is his appearance satisfactory in all circumstances? Has he acquired the grace to fit among the friends of the Boss and associates? He must ask himself these questions, as they are being asked by the Boss, as he moves forward in his demand for service from the Courtier.

First accompaniments are normally with the Boss —
alone. If there is comfort here, then accompaniment
with friends is in order. Confidence assured, a visit
to the family is forthcoming. To the house for a few
drinks after work; with the wife for dinner in some
restaurant; a shared weekend day on the golf course
or tennis court; then, an invitation to dinner at the
Boss' home. This progression is not iron-clad in the
sense listed but certainly will follow some pattern of
need for assurance of ability to assimilate into the
Boss' realm of personal activities.

The Courtier who joins the Boss has moved beyond
the Errand Boy category, yet will be used for the
purpose when it entails matters of greater significance.
Having entered the personal life of the Boss, he can
be of greater service. Knowledge of the Boss' family
and friends permits his use for errands of a very
personal nature. Gifts for wife and family can be
acquired by the Courtier. Assistance in obtaining information on vacation locations, car purchase, home
improvement, schools or colleges for children, jobs
for friends, all offer opportunity for the Courtier to
render service. With each satisfactory effort, the value
of the Courtier becomes more refined and necessary
to a Boss whose time is more efficiently utilized in
his function as leader of the organization that supports
them both.

As the time and frequency of joining with the Boss
increases, the knowledge of the Courtier increases,
knowledge of what procedures make the organization
effectively work. The Courtier is raised by association
to a position of adviser, or at the least to one who
becomes a sounding board for the Boss' ideas and
future plans. Such position demands of the Courtier
integrity and discretion. It also generates among the

peers of the Courtier, feelings of uncertainty regarding his friendship, and will among many generate dislike...and among a few, hate — the evident result of power.

A USEFUL PARALLEL

There is a close relationship between the Courtier and the Salesman. Experience in either practice is most helpful in the alternate pursuit.

The trained Salesman, one who has been exposed to the territory, will know his customers as personalities, each to be treated as individuals and offered service unique to his personal preference. Knowledge of the type demanded for successful practice, comes with exposure and awareness. Study and memory are necessary tools.

The game of personal contact, practiced with controlled banter, opens more doors for a Salesman than any product offering. To establish comfort, certainly the most demanded entre' into any discussion, is the Salesman's first effort. To accomplish a level of comfort, the adversary must be given complimentary offerings or statements of heroic reflection on past performance.

An attitude of fraternal well-being must be established to lend ease to the pursuit of the objective at hand. The accomplished Salesman has mastered this art and practices it with nonchalance. People are his tools, and to the needs of people he directs his weaponry.

The Courtier must acquire the same knowledge of his adversaries. In a sense, he is selling — no less than the Salesman. His product is not one of manufacture nor service, but his own future. His customers, if we can use the term in this context, are his bosses — the bosses he must satisfy and serve, if he is to attain the end to which his effort is directed. Not the accomplishment of the mechanical task his credentials reflect — this is concluded as foregone — but his mere presence on the job. He must sell his value as a partner in a system that demands total commitment. To offer or be willing to sacrifice less than a total measure, precludes even the sight of the winner's circle. Mastery of the rules — and the rules are in place — demands study and awareness that give light to the path that is to be followed. If a change in personality is demanded, a change in personal conversational adaptability, the aspiring Courtier will not only observe the need but will accept it and make the change in his armament that will permit continuance of the battle. Shy not away from the term battle, as recognition of its reality is possibly the first and most necessary pre-requisite to attainment of success.

The battle concept must be accepted. Within the Courtier's environment, whether it be office, factory, laboratory, government facility, educational institution, or any other workplace, a battle is raging on two fronts. The first is the battle of the full army of employees for the pursuit of the objectives of the operation. The second is the battle between the troops of the operational army for individual prominence. It is within this second combat zone that the Courtier must shine forth, with the results of pre-planned tactics, to attain the level of accomplishment that is offered to any who take up the burden.

As with the Salesman, the Courtier sees clearly the reward for effort and goes after it with a singleness of purpose, letting not the feelings or criticism of companions or comrades interfere. The satisfaction of success is too great a challenge to be inhibited by those who stand by and cry for want of reward or know not how to proceed. They are to be left standing — suffering their own deficiency.

Castiglione considered the knightly attributes of courage, horsemanship and skill at arms as requisites for the true courtier. Probably this unknown knight in Carpaccio's painting possessed these admirable qualities.